PRAISE FOR ASTRID

This Morning ITV - Astrid says we should all love our bodies. And what's more, she can tell you how to do it!

Woman's Own - Astrid is perfect proof that body image is all About believing in yourself

Irish Examiner - Refreshingly honest...will teach you how to Live your life in the now!

Slimmer, Healthier, Fitter - Combining motivation and upbeat advice, it's A good way to remind yourself that, actually you're Pretty fantastic after all!

Sunday Express - "Astrid Longhurst is tanned and toned and sexy – because that's the way you feel if you feel good about yourself!"

L A McCarthy - "Romancing your Body, is the ultimate book to learn how to fall in love with your body and your life. Astrid delivers a breathtaking intimate insight into what it means to create a loving relationship with yourself. It is the most inspirational, uplifting and transformational book of its time. Astrid shares her own journey and body struggles with humour, passion, warmth and amazing coaching tips, exercises and techniques for you to do the same. A must read for everyone who has ever struggled with their own body image, or who just needs a little more self love and tenderness towards themselves".

T Sullivan - "I went to one of Astrid's life & Body Confidence Coaching workshops six months ago. It wasn't life coaching – **it was life saving!** Thank you so much for helping me turn my life around. I've stopped dieting and started living! I couldn't have done it without you! I highly recommend Romancing your body, its like a workshop in book format and the results are extraordinary!"

J.M McCarthy - "I eat when I'm physically hungry! It's a miracle!!! The chapter on Romancing your body with food has completely changed my life. Read it!"

J. Gordon – I know what I am truly hungry for – a life less ordinary, a life that I can live in and speak my truth. Thank you Astrid for your compassion and gentle strength. Your book is a godsend and a miracle!"

M. Lacey – "Romancing your body has taught me to love my body! After 42 years of hating my body and always finding fault in how I looked I can honestly say that I love my body! It's a very special feeling to be able to look at me in the mirror and smile. The "knock on" effects are huge! I eat when I'm hungry, cry when I'm sad, laugh when I'm overjoyed and rest when I'm tired. They sound like simple things but believe me they were the most difficult for me to do! I never honoured who I was or kept my own promises. It was always about other people. I came last on my list of people to love and care about! Today, my blood pressure is normal, my weight is lower than it's ever been. I feel alive, healthy and happy. I'm real, rather than the ghost I used to be in my own life! Thank you for helping me make the connection!"

S. Fielding - “I think I might be around to see my grandchildren grow up now! At the age of 67 I am just learning how to say “Yes” to what I truly want and “No” to what I don’t! You’re never too old to change. Thank you for writing Romancing your body and bless you for helping me to finally “get it!”

ROMANCING YOUR BODY

HOW TO FALL DEEPLY, PASSIONATELY AND WILDLY IN LOVE WITH YOUR BODY AND YOUR LIFE!

ASTRID LONGHURST

Created with Vellum

HOW TO FALL DEEPLY, PASSIONATELY AND WILDLY IN LOVE WITH YOUR BODY AND YOUR LIFE!

Discover the seven soul body promises that will radically transform the way you feel!

- Stop putting your life "on hold" and commit to YOU.
- Make every day a love affair from the heart & embark on the most deeply fulfilling relationship of a lifetime – the one with YOU.
- Discover how to keep every promise you make to you and why it matters.
- Turn every day into a date with the Universe.
- Discover just how good your body can feel and why loving yourself is the most self-caring thing you can do for others.
- Break FREE from pain, shame and body doubt.
- Move out of your head and into your body.

- Discover what it is that you are truly hungry for.
- Romance your body & fall in love with your life.

DEDICATION

This book is dedicated to every BODY!

With Love

INTRODUCTION

Life – the greatest love affair of all time!

If life was a love affair and the way that we expressed and experienced this love and passion was through our body then I have to admit that my body love story would read more like a torrid melodrama than a passionate romance. My own relationship with my body has been nothing short of an epic drama. I have experienced the highs and the lows, the sweetness and the sorrow and still my body and I are together. I have to admit that I am surprised. If I was my body I think I would have left many years ago. I wouldn't have put up with the kind of abuse that I inflicted on my poor sweet body all through the years. My body is a testament to the extraordinary power of unconditional and often times unsupported and unrequited love. And I have to say, right here and now that I am so very grateful, humbled and delighted that we are still together and we live to breathe another day. Peace and love now reign in my life. I have learned how to give and also how to receive. I am a much kinder, calmer and enriched woman because of the teachings of my beloved body. Only my body and my relationship with it and my life could form and inform the woman that I am today. The woman who can sit here and write with love about her dearest and most precious friend and ally in the whole world – my gorgeous, beautiful, fabulous and extraordinary body. I am in love! I have been in love for a long time now and it's the real thing. An authentic love that springs from my heart and sparkles through my veins. I know that my body is "the one" I have been searching for all of these years and it feels wild and crazy that the body I have now is the one that I've always had but just never noticed it before. It feels awesome to be able to walk out in the world proudly owning my beautiful body. I dress it up now and seek to make it happy. Once we wore just the dark shadow cover up clothes to make us seem invisible as we skulked along the side streets of our days. Head down don't make eye contact. Just try to get to your destination without too much attention! Ah, safe at home – now where did I put that packet of biscuits?

Today, we laugh together as we choose what *feelings* we want to express and create. Is it the bright pink and turquoise chiffon kaftan that flows and whispers through our every movement? Or maybe it's the white ruffled maxi dress that sweeps me up in passion with every step I take? I open the sliding door of my wardrobe and I scan the clothes all yearning to get their chance to be worn be me. I smile, breathe deeply, close my eyes and say to these wild clothes horses eager to be let out of the stalls – "Dress me" Opening my eyes I spot the lilac off the shoulder jumper which aches to be reunited with the black skirt and heavy black sparkly boho belt I bought years ago but never wore! Oh what joy! Who would have thought that just choosing what clothes to wear could be such a happy and loving experience? As someone who (in the past) would have been grateful for a tent to cover me up, this is one of the most delightful and fulfilling moments of my day. It's so simple and yet so satisfying. So ordinary and yet there is nothing ordinary about this because this is alchemy in action. Perhaps it sounds odd when I talk in terms of my body and me as a "we" but that's exactly what I feel now. It's no longer that dreadful empty feeling of disconnection or avoidance when I speak about my body – it is a feeling of inclusion and engagement.

This is what it means when you decide to fall in love with your beautiful body and come home to the *you* that you've always desired to be. This is LOVE IN ACTION! It is a love that is similar but quite unlike the love I have felt for another human being. It's deeply personal and quietly insistent that it is acknowledged every moment of every day. I cannot simply walk out of the door when I've had enough of me or when I'm feeling so low and fed up that all I want to do is run for the hills. No, this love is like super glue. It sticks to every part of me and holds me close. Tethered to my romantic soul that yearns to be seen, felt, desired, experienced, cherished, adored, lifted up and proclaimed to the world how gloriously beautiful this love is! And yet, I have spent what seems an eternity running from this all embracing passion. I have run so hard and escaped so many times into the shallow and tenuous embraces of those I thought loved me more or who would provide me a brief sanctuary from myself. I have run into the open glittering but sterile cold arms of my fridge begging it to help me through another torrid war that I have waged upon myself – upon my body. I have blamed my body for all of the things that I dare not address in my life or had the courage to meet. I should really have been an Olympic athlete for the miles I have spent running and the marathons I have endured trying desperately to find that place where peace resides and harmony is queen. And through all of it I have longed to stay. I have yearned to feel that aliveness that can only come from being fully engaged and in love with your life. I have ached to be present for the feelings that coursed through my soul. I have longed to fully inhabit the body I have and turn to me for the love I craved. My deepest desire was to be fully alive whilst I *am* alive. I have yearned to listen to the soft call of my tender flesh as it wrapped around my beautiful strong bones and invited me to stay awhile. I have longed with all of my heart to turn kindly eyes upon me and come "home" to the woman I am and the magnificent body I live in!

You can hide but you can't run!

Why is it so hard to simply be where you are and love the moment you discover yourself in? Why is it so difficult to caress your body with love and appreciation and love every single curve, bump, dimple and pimple? Why is it so tough to face your fear – to look into its scared little wizened face, cup your hands around its wrinkly aged cheeks and tell it you love it anyway? It's only my fear – what can be so bad about it? And yet I ran. Ran away from my body, myself, my dreams, my gifts and my life. The irony of course is that you can run as far as you like but you will always be with you. There isn't a place on the earth that you can hide from your authentic Self and your magnificent soul. I did a fabulous job of subduing my feelings and letting me off the "hook" of my life. I always had the greatest reasons why I couldn't achieve my dreams, write that book, go to that party, take that trip or be up for all of that living that others somehow seemed to do so easily. I used to wonder how other people lived their lives without the constant companionship and pre-planned escape route of food and self doubt and harm. How did they cope with all of the things that life brought them and still stay standing to face another day. This always amazed me. All of those moments where they could have chosen to bolt or abandon themselves and yet they stood proudly and courageously by their own side. How wonderful to love yourself so much that you don't abandon yourself when you need you the most!

However for many people life isn't a love affair – it's something to get through – to be endured. I have coached thousands of people and the common thread that binds them all is that in some way, shape or form, they have vacated their life. There's no one "home" – they are not present any more. Some where at some time they walked away from their deepest dreams and ignored the tribal prayer of their heart, beating out it's powerful thumping drums of love and passion. I know this too - I lived this! It's no wonder that so many people say that they feel "lost." When we refuse to show up in our life, we *are* lost. We are lost to ourself. We have neglected the very core of our being and our connection with who we truly are. When we don't own our gifts, talents, joys and dreams we become lost. When we believe that we are not good enough, we lose who we are because the truth is that we've *always* been good enough. When we believe that our negative and self-limiting thoughts are true we drift away from the beauty of the truth of whom we authentically are, which is magnificent beyond measure. The result is that we begin to search for ways to fill those empty spaces and cracks we feel inside and instead of turning to meet ourself with love and compassion, we accept substitutes for a life less lived. We may fill up the emptiness we feel inside with copious amounts of food, alcohol, over working, drugs, sex, toxic relationships, gambling, computer games, endless hours watching TV or scanning Facebook for what everyone else is doing in their lives. We simply try to avoid ever meeting ourselves on a daily basis. Many people focus externally on other people as their way to leave their body and their life. They spend their precious hours wondering what others may (or may not) be thinking about them. They "people please" to such an extent that there's no time left in the day to please themselves. They may fill every waking hour with busyness and running into the next moment avoiding the very one they are living in. Such is our desire to leave our lives. Such is our wish to abandon our body.

One of my clients told me that she hadn't had a shower for over 25 years. Although she had *physically* been in the shower, she never experienced the delicious scent of her shower cream or the cascading hot water that flowed over her body. Her mind was always too busy worrying about what the day would bring, how much she had to do and just making it through to the end of the day. One of the first ways that she began to love herself and re-appear in her life was to simply be present in her morning shower.

I, too was good at escaping! My body provided the quickest and the easiest route out. It was the surest way that I could step back from my life and disappear into oblivion. Instead of feeling what I felt in the moment or communicating what I really needed and desired, I simply left my life via my body. My body provided the exit door through which I repeatedly bolted for the hills. My personal form of escape was food. The more I ate the quicker I left the world around me, disappearing into a haze of forgotten dreams, promises and numbed out feelings. This was my nirvana. This was my very own way that I could stop time and just fall into the comforting coma that food gave me. My body was the thing that I blamed for my unhappiness. If I were slimmer, I would be more lovable, successful, happier, more attractive, desirable etc. The list of my body beliefs were endless in their capacity to keep me away from loving my body and away from living my authentic life.

There are many ways we can choose to escape from the greatest romance of all time. It doesn't have to be food. There are many ways that we choose to leave and reject ourselves and become seduced by those empty lovers that promise us the world but always fail to deliver. They show up under all kinds of different guises. We've probably met them all at different times in our life. We slide precariously into the welcoming warm, tipsy and mellow arms of our alcohol lover. We fantasise about coming home every night and disappearing into the sweet liquid that warms our veins, stirs our hearts, clouds our brains and tells us that it's all okay. We nod our heads silently as we open yet another bottle and pour our heart and soul into its slippery wet and aromatic contents.

Tomorrow, we promise ourselves, tomorrow we will drink a little less and live a little more. We toss back our wild and wanton curls, lift our defiant chins to the deepening and darkening velvet sky and just like Scarlet O Hara in "Gone with the wind" we whisper to ourselves convincingly, that "After all, tomorrow is another day" forgetting that tomorrow will be exactly like the day before and the day before that! We busy ourselves with pleasing anyone who crosses our path, hoping perhaps for a little love or gratitude for all that we have done for them. A dear and beautiful friend of mine moved me deeply when he told me how he would just love to be noticed and appreciated by his partner of ten years. He did everything he could to please his love. "I'm not asking for much," he would say. "Even a pat on the head would be enough. Even the dog gets more attention than I do!" We tell ourselves that we'll leave work on time and not put in another two hours of unasked and unpaid filing, hating the way we keep having these one night stands of unrequited work in the office but desperately seeking the brief hit of acknowledgment and appreciation that they may bring. Oh yes, our secret loves can show up in many ways as they call us away from spending time with the most precious person in our Universe – us!

A fridge named "Harry!"

For me my knight in shining armour and greatest secret love and escape was my fridge! He was always there standing tall, upright, white, shiny, powerful and throbbing with a low hum of pure pleasure and anticipation. He was a God! My God! He could spirit me away in the briefest of moments – up, up and away as I searched for some sweetness and comfort in his brightly lit smile! My saviour! I called him Harry. Not a glamorous name for a knight in fridge's clothing but accessible, real and a bit earthy. I couldn't have gone for a Sir Lancelot or even an Arthur. I toyed with the idea of calling him D'Artagnan from the four musketeers, but knew I could never show him the side of me that wasn't in control, perfect and fabulous. But Harry – well Harry didn't mind what I looked like or how I felt. He just was always pleased to see me no matter what time of day or night. Harry – my fridge. Harry my own little bite size fairytale. How beautiful he looked – gleaming with excitement and giving me glimpses of all of the tantalising goodies inside his steely strong exterior. All I had to do was to let him in and say "YES" to all the pleasure he had to offer. My heart would quicken just at the thought of him. My pulse would race as I imagined the sweet light that would flicker on as I opened his arms and crawled into his all consuming (but rather cold) embrace. This was where I found unconditional love. Just my knight and me - my own secret holy grail of comfort. It was an affair that began as far back as I could remember. I knew it was toxic, I knew it wasn't doing me any good but I also knew that like many people who refuse to walk away from what hurts them into the arms of what loves them, that I was addicted. Who was I without my secret stash of sugar? What would it be like to live life naked – without the protective armour of my guilt, sorrow, frozen feelings and numbed out body? Standing in front of the open arms of my prince of frozen produce, I was safe. He asked no questions – I told plenty of lies but we seemed to knock along very happily, until the moment came when I realised that he didn't fulfil me any more. Nothing he seemed to offer me could satisfy me and I began looking elsewhere for what I was truly hungering for, what I really craved in my life. It wasn't anything he'd done. It was me; I just didn't want to accept substitutes anymore for feeling what I felt and living how I desired. The question was how could I live without him? What would it take for me not to turn to him when all around me felt like chaos and was too much to bear? How on earth could I feel the overwhelming feelings that I had tried so hard to silence for years? Would I die from too much pain, grief and fear? I didn't know how I would ever live without him, but I knew I had to try. I wondered, how on earth did people live so close to the surface? It was a question that haunted and called to me to find out. What would it be like to be FREE? What would it FEEL like to dance through my life instead of stumble? Maybe I could turn my stumbles into the dance? There was something within me that could *sense* how wonderful it could be and how fabulous I could feel. Slowly my hunger began to change from food and wanting to numb out my life into a burning desire to be here for every moment. It was this inner calling and whispering that began to consume my days. And what of my beloved Harry? Well, these days it's a more real and authentic relationship that we have. He's still as strong and gorgeous as ever but I only visit him now when I am truly hungry. It works on every level. He only contains the food that really fulfils me and I only see him when I truly desire his company. It's more honest. It's real and it's deeply satisfying. I have a sneaky feeling that somewhere deep down in the nuts and bolts of his fridge-like being that this arrangement rather suits him as much as it does me.

Falling in love again

So this is what this book is all about – romancing your body. It's about falling headlong, deeply, madly, wildly and passionately in love with YOU, your BODY and your life. It's about wanting something new. It's about being ready to be seduced by the you that you may have seen flirtatious glimpses of but never known. It's about wanting to have an affair with your body, your heart, your mind and your soul. No, it's MORE than an affair! It's about having the greatest romance the world has ever seen! It's about creating and delighting in the full blown bodice ripping, toe tingling, all consuming, breath taking, heart stopping and achingly glorious most wonderful love and life of all time! It's about opening yourself up to a sweet, tender and full-bodied love! A love that can only be given and be received by YOU! If you are reading these words it's highly likely that you're ready to indulge in the most fulfilling, hedonistic, passionate and wildly satisfying romance of your mind, body, heart and soul. You may have become tired with treating yourself badly in the hopes that you'll feel good. You may have tried every trick in the book that there is and have simply come to one flawless conclusion – that loving yourself, your body and your life is the only path to true happiness, joy and inner peace. You may be experiencing the same feeling as I did when all that truly mattered was experiencing a more loving and deeply fulfilling relationship with yourself. A relationship that will take you to the edge of everything that you ever thought you could be and feel and demand that you jump in and experience it all!

It's not for the faint hearted – loving yourself so passionately is a wild and deeply radical act. It's something that is not taught in our society for fear that you will love yourself too much or not love others enough. Such flawed notions put across by those who have never melted into their own loving and tender embrace or heard the voice of their soul whispering "Go on my love – you can do it. I am so proud of you!" Their fear is that we might become too arrogant – too full of ourselves or conceited if we would but dare look into the mirror and smile at what we saw lingering there, waiting to be adored. So instead, we turn away, missing the glimmer of sadness in our own eyes as we favour an approach that dismisses the awesome epic beauty that stands before us. And we are EPIC! All of us! There is not one human being on the face of this earth that is not glorious and magnificent beyond belief and who deserves the greatest love of all time – Your own!

Romancing your body is about making every moment with you the most beautiful, authentic, loving, kind, compassionate and sensuous experience. From awakening in the morning to going back to sleep at the end of each day, loving your body brings the romance back into your life on every level and in every moment. We have lost the art of truly showing ourselves love and showing up authentically in our own lives. This book brings that lost art back into focus. We often say that we love our bodies but then find ourselves pushing our body harder and harder in a workout, going beyond where our body needs or wants to go. We say we love our body and then break our promise to get more sleep or stop eating so much sugar. We proclaim to love who we are and then judge and criticise our self when something goes wrong. Love defines our lives and is expressed in the detail and the moments of every minute. The best way to express and experience this love is through your amazing body.

Romancing your body invites you to really *show up in your life* by keeping your promises to your amazing body. Not just when every one else is around or watching but in those quiet subtle moments of your day when it's just you and your body. How do you treat yourself when no one else is around? What kind of things do you say to yourself when it's just you and your body? What do you eat when no one else is looking? What do you wear? What do you say, think, believe and do? I realised that so often I would treat my body one way when I was in company but when I was alone with me, the gloves came off and it didn't seem to matter how I treated myself or my body. Eating out socially was a prime example. I would go out to dinner and order what looked good and what made *me* look good. Loads of salad, fruit, low calorie deserts and herbal tea. It looked as if I must have been the healthiest person on the planet. However, when I got home I would "break out" into a frenzy of chocolate, crisps, ice cream, full fat cheese and copious amounts of bread and butter. Feeling fully satiated I would fall into a food "coma" and collapse into bed for what usually was the worst nights sleep I could have. This wasn't love. This was extreme bullying and disrespect. The truest test of love lies in how we treat ourselves when we are alone with ourself. When it's just you and your beautiful body what will you do, how will you live, what will you say to yourself and how much love will you give yourself? Are you the same person you show to the world when you're behind closed doors and it's just you with you? There is a saying "street angel, house devil," which highlights how someone always comes across as just "perfect" and doing the "right" thing on the outside but once inside closed doors the reverse is the truth and all hell can break loose. It's the same for many people who have suffered or are suffering with the relationship with their body. On the outside they may wear a "mask" or "body armour" to hide their true feelings and come across as being *seen* to be doing all the right things. However, once alone with only themselves the truth of their feelings come out as they systematically wage war upon their body. This war can take many shapes and forms. From over exercising, compulsive eating, hurtful, critical thoughts, under eating, lack of restful sleep, alcohol abuse, chronic lack of self-care or allowing themselves to be hurt or abused by others. It's a case of body angel, body devil as on the outside they are all things to every *other* body whilst on the inside they repeatedly fail to show up for themselves. The key is to bring both sides into a state of body integrity whereby the person can discover who they authentically are and begin to feel safe enough to express this externally and internally. If you were dating someone who consistently broke their word and failed to keep their promises how would you feel? Would you feel safe, valued and cherished in the relationship? Would you trust your partner or would shadows of doubt begin to creep in and ultimately undermine the entire relationship?

Keeping your own Promises

Romancing your body shows you how to fall in love with ALL of you. Not just the bits that you deem acceptable but also every single part of your body. It's about unconditional passionate love that accepts all of you whenever and however you are. It is a book full of the most delicious ways to love your body, honour your self and fall in love with your life – every day of your life. The book invites you to embark on the most loving and fulfilling relationship of your life – the one with your body, heart, mind and soul. It is written in the form of seven soul body promises that make up the core of every loving and successful relationship. Each promise asks you to make a commitment to your body, heart and soul and allow these promises to truly show up in your life as you fall more deeply and authentically in love with all of you!

One of the hardest things to do is to keep our own promises and commit to ourselves. We will often go out of the way to make sure that we don't let another person down. We wouldn't dream of not getting that work project in on time or spending time with a loved family member because we promised that we would. However when it comes to keeping our *own* promises we often are dismally neglectful. We make it okay to stay up way too late although we've said we will get to bed earlier. We come up with endless excuses as to why we won't bother taking some time out. We put off doing what we *know* would bring us happiness by spinning the story that we don't have the time, energy, money or talent. We make it acceptable to fill our body with junk food and tell ourselves that we'll be "good" tomorrow or after the weekend or Christmas or whatever happens to be coming up that we don't want to be "good" for! We keep our lives endlessly on "hold" like the phone that keeps ringing; we ignore it believing that if it's important the person will ring back.

If not now – when?

And so we miss the greatest and most urgent calls of our soul and opportunities of our life. The soul always wants to be answered, to be heard and it's desires to be expressed. My question to myself was if not now, when? When would I stop pretending that I didn't hear the phone ringing and ignore the calling of my soul? When would I turn around and face *me* in the mirror and realise the love I was seeking has always been waiting patiently there? When was I going to stop pretending that junk food fulfilled me when all it did was to medicate and numb me? When did I make this an acceptable way to live with me? How did I make hurting me and not believing in me a valid way of living? And this is the question that I am asking *you* right now – if not now when? You can put your life on the back burner for an eternity making excuses and giving yourself plausible reasons why you shouldn't fall in love with you and adore your precious body. Does it bring you happiness? Does it give you everything you've always desired? Is this the way that you truly want to live? I am sure that you are far too wonderful, magnificent and gorgeous to spend another day away from your beautiful Self. I spent far too long waiting to live, waiting to feel whole, valued, acceptable and loved. I hung around the edges of my skin, not wanting to be associated with the body I had. I made excuses for my body and was ashamed of how I looked. I made empty promises that once I was thin I would finally let myself love me, finally do all the things I said I would do. I spent many years trying to be the person that other people wanted me to be and ultimately there's simply no point. It doesn't work on any level. If you think that trying to please someone else by saying "YES" when your entire body, mind and spirit is shouting "No" will bring you joy – you are mistaken.

Saying "YES" to YOU

When you say "YES" to you, your body and your life, you can give of yourself freely and expansively. You know how to set loving boundaries and truly care for yourself and others. Imagine waking up every morning feeling the greatest happiness and joy that you are YOU! Imagine every day as a love affair and your greatest intention is to bring your body pleasure, joy and happiness. Since every day brings us another chance to connect with and love ourselves "Romancing your body," asks the questions – will you commit to loving yourself today? Will you keep your own promises and allow yourself to be the fullest expression of who you truly are? Will you still love you when you are tired or your body is wracked with pain?

Healthy, successful and sustainable relationships are built and developed from the promises that we keep, the love that we give & receive, the actions we take, the thoughts we think and the authenticity and integrity that we bring. It is all about how much we are able to show up and commit to the people we love and care about in our lives. When you give your love, commitment, passion and trust to YOU, every single other relationship you will ever have is strengthened, deepened and amplified. How do you do this? By keeping the promises of love to yourself. When you keep your word to your body, you embody your love and commitment. Every single cell in your body experiences your love and truth. No longer do you feed yourself empty commitments or platitudes to keep you quiet. No longer will you accept the unacceptable and make it okay to hurt yourself or believe that you are not good enough. Love becomes the one true way that you begin to steer your soul body into a galaxy of infinite possibilities and potential. Quantum science has shown us the incredible effect that our words, thoughts, actions, beliefs and energy has on creating an inner environment of peace, health, happiness and fulfilment. Romancing your body shows you how to embody this science by consciously choosing to fall in love with you. Think of this book as a love affair between the pages. It's a way of living that invites you to fall in love with every second of your life as it unfolds moment by moment. It's about passionate, dreamy, awesome living that asks you to commit to the deepest experience of loving you, your body and your amazing life. Romancing your body is a relationship that never ends – it's eternal, deeply fulfilling and radically transforming.

This book is for EVERY BODY!

There are seven promises. Every one is a commitment and a practice that you pledge to make to your body every day to bring more love and romance to your body. You are invited to gradually increase more love every single day of your life until you are simply living and loving your body and keeping your promises in the fullest way possible.

Start with one body promise and focus on this until it becomes a natural and enjoyable part of your day. Build your promises and your commitment to yourself by adding in all of the seven promises until you realise that you wouldn't dream of being any other way with your body. Begin with just one promise and begin to practice until you get really good at it. If you forget to keep your promise simply recognise that fact and return to your commitment as soon as you can. Don't beat yourself up for not keeping it – that's not love. That's unkindness. Just be aware of where you need to focus more on you and strengthen your commitment to love you more. Like every relationship, romancing your body takes time, practice, commitment, willingness and a longing for a love affair that is always asking you to grow and become MORE of the amazing, authentic you that you are!

My deepest wish is that this book will inspire you to fall in love with YOUR body and your life. That you take YOU by the hand as you twirl yourself around the dance floor and say, "Come on, let's rock!" My deepest passion is that you embark on the most wonderful relationship in the history of all time – the relationship with you – mind, body, heart and soul. And that every page will bring you some note of wisdom, comfort, understanding or laughter. My dream is that you will begin to see your body as the beautiful miracle you have been given in which to express and enjoy your most amazing life.

1

WHAT IF YOU JUST DECIDED TO LOVE YOU?

Dear Beautiful You
How can you not love me?
When we were born to be together!
Your one and only....body xx

WHAT IF EVERY moment of every day brought you a chance to fall more deeply in love with YOU? What if the ordinary, more mundane moments of your life could be turned into magical, divine moments of pure unadulterated passionate pleasure and presence? What if you vowed to love your body and make a commitment to loving YOU all the days of your life?

How would your life be different? What could be happening that may not be happening now? Love changes every thing. It is the most powerful force in the entire Universe. When you make a conscious choice to love your body, you transform your life. Something extraordinarily magical happens when you decide to love your body – life falls in love with you! Your entire landscape and experience of what it means to be fully alive changes! Every single moment of your life becomes sweeter, deeper, more blissful and peaceful. Like the most glorious blossoming rose, your own authentic beauty and uniqueness expands, shines and radiates in the sun's golden warmth and light of its rays.

Love at its core is a commitment. A promise that you will be there, that you will listen and do everything in your power to express the love that you feel. Love is a verb – it's a "doing" word. Any love that promises one thing but does another is not love – it's neglect. It's an empty word and a broken promise that leaves you feeling unfulfilled and under valued. True love shows up in every way it can. Like the indomitable spirit of the flower that manages to push its way through the cracks in the concrete to bloom unashamedly, love finds its way through the crevices and pores of our being until it can pour out of our heart and bask in the light of our awesome soul. Love is the body's currency. It's what it lives by and thrives on. For your body to thrive it demands that you love it. Unlike many other relationships where you can walk away from what doesn't work, the relationship with your body insists that you stay and work this one out! Your body will only be silent for so long. It will endure being ignored or treated badly up to a point but sooner or later it will make it's presence known and cry out to have it's needs met. Love, tenderness, appreciation, kindness, compassion and gratitude are the qualities your body thrives on. No one but our dear sweet body could ever teach us what it means to be fully alive, flourishing and nourished in this world. No one but our beautiful body can ever give us the joy of experiencing and feeling the joy of what it means to take care of the most precious gift we will ever have – the skin we live in! The body is an insistent partner – it always demands true love. It cannot be fobbed off with the odd nod of appreciation in its direction. It knows when you are cheating and will always bring you back to face the moment of truth. Your body adores you and is in rapture with its own beloved beauty. Every single little part of your being – every bump and lump, freckle and speckle. Your body is in awe of its own magnificence and rightly so – it is a work of forever changing art. Your body always desires to know how much you adore it too. It seeks your love in every moment of every day. It's questions are always, "How much living can we enjoy together?" It consistently whispers, "Show me you love me"

Love is saying "I DO" to YOU!

True love is found and discovered in all of those tiny sweet delicious moments that you share with the being of your body. It is found in the simplest things - the cup of tea, the heady heat of the morning shower, the food you eat, the words you say, the clothes you wear, the work you do, the lazy afternoons you spend just soaking up the sun or reading in the shade. Your body laps up joy like the ocean caresses the shore. The wonderful thing is that life brings us endless moments of infinite pleasure. Love shows up and blusters through our life as the warm winds play and dance through our hair. Love lingers around the edges of someone's smile, their touch, their compassion and fills us up with affection. Love shows up in the way you move, the words you write, the songs you sing and the sparkle in your eyes. Love is also deeply discovered in those moments when the storm clouds roll in and your world seems shaken, unresolved, out of balance and too much to bear. Perhaps this is where our most enduring love and commitment with truly loving ourself is found. When everything feels overwhelming and out of control, when your life feels less like a loving relationship and more like an ongoing divorce or separation, this is where true authentic love shows up the most. The deepest love is found when you choose to stand *with* you rather than abandon you. When you stand your ground with courage and conviction and make a decision that no matter what else may be happening, you'd rather be here with you than anywhere else in the world. That's LOVE! This is also where true glorious, bold and epic transformation occurs. The temptation to run from ourselves in our lives are all too seductive. However, the whole point of living your most fabulous life isn't about escaping or avoiding how you feel, it's about becoming more fully alive every day of your life. It's about bringing out all of those unused, unrealised parts of you and sharing your potential, passion and personal power with the world. The world needs you to treasure yourself so that it may share in all of the gifts that you bring.

When you allow yourself to become distracted instead of paying yourself attention, you side step your inner most callings. When you stop taking baby steps to follow your dreams you "forget" who you truly are. When you refuse to feel your emotions or be consciously present for whatever is arising within you, there is a disengagement that seeks to separate you with you! If you behaved this way in a relationship it would surely suffer or be difficult to sustain. Imagine that your partner continually asked you to spend a little more time with them, to listen to what they had to say, accompany them on some special outing and enjoy the moments of life. And instead of taking the time to be fully present in their company you ignored every word. You shrugged off every opportunity and preferred instead to lose yourself in negative thoughts, critical judgements, over work and generally avoided ever being close to them. There would be (at the very least) a disconnect in the relationship.

A call to Action

Romancing your body is a call to action! A gentle and loving reminder of who you really are. It's an invitation to truly show up in your own life in your amazing body and declare to the world that YES! You absolutely adore the very bones of YOU! The Shamans say that there is only one illness or disease in this life. It is the sense of separation or disconnection from *all* of who we are. Today, more than ever before, our minds, our emotions, our relationships, and our bodies are out of kilter. We know it, but we tend to ignore it until something happens that wakes us up from our self-induced amnesia! We may face a worrying diagnosis, a broken relationship, the death of a loved one, or we may find that we are simply less able to function harmoniously in everyday life. And so the real journey of life begins...the journey *home* to the core of our being, our magnificence and our greatest joy, health, happiness and purpose! To truly heal, thrive and grow we need to fall in love again and take care of our body, mind, heart, soul and the beautiful planet that we live within. No longer separate or disconnected we will spread our wings and soar on life's buoyant and bountiful currents. We will trust the direction of the winds of change and we will steer by the feelings of our heart.

The body's truth

Our bodies speak the clearest truth about who we are, what we love and what our purpose is in this life. They cannot lie. When you turn to your body for your answers, you will find them instantly. How do you know? Because the language of your soul speaks through your body in thousands of different feelings, tugs, calls, whoops, hollers, truth shivers and whispers. Your mind can try to convince you that what you are doing is the right thing but your body will always know your real truth. There is nothing so beautiful as a body that has found it's authentic voice and a soul who has been fully embodied.

2

THE STIRRING OF A LOVE AFFAIR

Dear beautiful you
Just indulge me on this one...
Put your right hand on your left shoulder
And your left hand on your right shoulder
Okay, now squeeze together tightly.
Thanks – I just needed a hug!
Love from your body! x

"I want a divorce from myself!"

Reasons:
Betrayal
Abuse – verbal, physical and emotional
Failure to commit
Broken vows and promises
Mental cruelty

These were the words I found scribbled inside one of my many journals I had kept over the years. I had forgotten I had written them. They continued... "I've been in a relationship with me all of my life and I've never fully committed to loving who I am!" Those words made me stop and think. I was fed up with the way that I consistently treated myself. I was so sick and tired of the endless battles I waged upon my body demanding that it was perfect. I had had enough of being the last person I truly loved and cared about in my life and I wanted something more. Intuitively I knew that there had to be a better, more magical, authentic way to live. I wanted something new! I was ready to be seduced by the me I'd only ever seen flirtatious glimpses of but never really known. I wanted an affair....no damn it I wanted more than an affair. I wanted a life long fabulous, passionate, glorious romance with ME! I wanted to woo myself and get excited by the thought of seeing me rather than try to avoid all contact with me. I wanted to spend ages getting dressed up for me and feel delighted in how I looked. I wanted to hold me in my arms and tell me that I loved me and I wanted to know and believe that it was true.

I wanted to sweep me up in the whirlwind of my desires and set my heart beating wildly at all the living and the fun that we could have. I wanted to get up early and stay out late. I wanted to give *me* all that my life could offer. I wanted to take me out and be proud of who I was with. I wanted to be excited just by the thought of me! And I wanted to go up to everyone I met and say "aren't you FABULOUS! AND I AM FABULOUS TOO!" I wanted to stand up for me, fight for me, be proud of me, champion and celebrate me. I wanted to play, laugh, dance and have fun with me. I wanted to get to know this wonderful woman. And more than anything I wanted to make her my own! I wanted to stare into my own eyes and love ME unconditionally.

I wanted to take me by the hand and run full pelt into the wildness of my heart, and tango across the expanse of my dreams. I wanted to whisper softly to me as I fell asleep, safe within my body and cradled by the Universe. I wanted to hear the things I had to say and say the things I longed to hear. I wanted to fall in love again and again...with me, with my life and with the world. I wanted to keep every promise I made to myself and make my word my bond. I wanted to honour my commitment to me and live the life my soul hungered for. I wanted to fall in love with me – wholeheartedly, unreservedly, fully, deeply, madly, truly! I wanted to say “I DO” to the woman I AM”

Passionate Living!

Reading these words in my diary rekindled something within me that took hold and ignited a passion that I had kept buried for years. I realised that I wanted to love me, run wild with me, and feel my life through every vein and every artery. I longed to fully LIVE whilst I was ALIVE! I wanted to turn every day of my life into a date with the Universe and commit to it with all my heart! My body ached to wear taffeta ball gowns and dance along sun drenched beaches. I suddenly longed to wear gypsy skirts dripping with romance and a touch of Organza. I began to spend more time barefoot. I wanted to eat what I loved and loved what I ate. Instead of pictures of the emaciated models that once dominated my teenage bedroom walls, I began to cut out pictures of strawberry cupcakes and stuck them on my computer where I could feast on them daily. I started creating scrapbooks full of pictures of roses, endless white beaches and turquoise blue seas. I hankered after shimmering sunsets and hazy gossamer moons. I wanted to taste the banquet of life and sit at its table knowing that I could choose anything I desired. I wanted to laugh in the face of calories and kick those “points” to the curb! I yearned to TASTE my life and wrap myself up in its flavour. I began to see me in every picture I saw. I was the white wolf and the soaring eagle. I was the shifting shimmering sand and the clearest turquoise sea. I was the stormy skies, the softest rain and the balmy golden evenings of summer. I was eternal. My soul was hungering – my body was shifting. I was awakening!

This book was written from my own deep personal need to

connect with and love my body. Refusing to love my body was the way that I denied myself the joy of being fully present in my life. From as far back as I can remember I always had a toxic relationship with my body - with myself. Actually it wasn't so much of a relationship as more of a dictatorship. I blamed my body for all that was wrong in my life. I thought that if my body were like the "perfect" fabulous bodies I hungered for in the glossy magazines that my life would be perfect too. I refused to listen to my body. I didn't want to hear. I didn't want to know. I thought that if I followed the diets, hated myself enough, ran the miles, sweated the pain then I would be rewarded with the "perfect" body and therefore the "perfect" life.

Like many other women I have lost and re-gained the same weight over and over again. Why? Because although we may be able to control ourselves, our appetites and our hungers for a short amount of time and lose some weight - the truth is that nothing fundamental had changed in our relationships with ourselves. The other fundamental and sacred truth is that it is NEVER about the weight, it is always and forever about our relationship with food, and more importantly with who we are. And, like many other women instead of focusing on the size of my life, I chose to give all my attention and energy to the size of my hips! I blamed my body for the life I believed I wasn't good enough to live. I spent much of my life waiting and hiding. Waiting for my life to begin when I was slim enough, perfect enough – good enough. Hiding from the sounds of my life slipping by like the drip drip of water that wears away the stone, I made it okay in my mind that it's an acceptable trade off – No life until I'm "perfect!" That sounds reasonable! But it's not reasonable – it's NOT OKAY! It never has been and it never will be!

Body Ghosts

Whether you're big, small, old or young, when you don't love the skin you're in you spend most of your time outside of yourself. It's as if you've left your body and what you see is a ghost of the woman (or man) that you could be! Rather like the poor tormented lovesick Cathy in Wuthering heights, outside in the howling winds, banging on the window to be let in by Heathcliff, you turn a cold shoulder to yourself and deny you the greatest love of all - the chance to be loved fully and passionately by YOU! And whilst you may experience the passion of being loved by another, if you don't fall in love with yourself first, then it is difficult to give what you have never truly and authentically experienced. Not only do you then cheat yourself, but you cheat your partner too!

The world is full of ghosts today. We see them in the young and the old, the thin and the obese, and all the shapes and sizes in between. People who for all intents and purposes look as if they inhabit the bodies they walk around in. And whilst some of them may be fully present, most are fleeting shadows of the people that they are yet to become. They haven't made the connection that they are the most magnificent being this world has ever seen. They haven't looked in the mirror and fallen in love again and again with the radiant beauty and wonder reflected back at them. They haven't counted their freckles and exclaimed how many beauty spots they have! They haven't seen how sexy that scar on their upper lip makes them. They've failed to notice the way their smile lights up the Universe or the way they move is like a magic carpet ride! They block their creativity as they hunger for the day when they will feel as if they belong and when they are good enough. What they fail to realise is that day is here, that moment is NOW! That they are and always have been good enough. The lie was that they're not. We are so cavalier with our souls embodiment...we believe we have forever but what we fail to realise is that whilst our souls are eternal their unique expression in this body is limited.

You're just not that into you!

There's a great piece in the Television series "Sex and the city" where the girls are trying to convince their friend Miranda that her potential new love interest in her life will call. They make excuses for why he hasn't rung, emailed or been in contact. "He's busy, it's a good thing, it means he respects you, he's giving you time...don't worry - he'll call." The moment of revelation arises when one of the friends, (Carrie) asks her current romantic partner what he thinks. He says it straight and cuts through all of the reassuring excuses. "He's just not that into you!" The girls are horrified but the truth sinks in as they realise that if he WERE interested he would have called, he would have shown up and he would have made the effort! The same applies to the relationship that we have with our bodies. It's as if we're just not that into ourselves as we ignore our heart's whispers, fill our bodies with someone else's idea of what is right for us, placate ourselves with substitutes for the real thing - whether that's food, a real relationship or a life that we can call our own! We break our own promises again and again and all too often fail to show up in our own lives! It seems that we are just not that in to who we are!

The problem with this is that hundreds of thousands of people are walking around in bodies and lives that they dislike and disown. We are disconnected and alienated from the truth of our magnificence, of the miracles we all are. Children as young as four are becoming body conscious and can point out their "faults" I once overheard a five year old complaining about her "saddlebags" and that she wasn't going to eat chocolate anymore.

A recent survey showed that a staggering 94% of women think negatively about their bodies every fifteen minutes. Personally, I believe it's probably more like every couple of minutes!

Many focus on getting "out of their body" through food, drugs, alcohol, sex, overworking, denial, toxic relationships etc. However, the real secret is to get IN TO your body! When you tap in to your body's intelligence, listen to the wisdom sparkling through your arteries and strut to the sound of your synapses, you leave behind what is false and doesn't belong to you. You bypass the "should's" the "oughts" the "if only's" and the "what if's." You swagger past what is NOT meant for you and set a starlit supernova ride for your true north. You giggle as you eat foods that make you go "Yum" and live a soul-full life in a body you love! You blow a kiss to those who cry, "You can't!" as you blast them with puffs of love and say, "Yes, I can and so can you!" No longer a ghost or a pale expression of who you *could* be – you are EPIC! You are a full technicolour landscape – a glorious symphony of colours, sounds and feelings that flow through you, ideas that caress your capabilities and flood you with every excited particle of the Universe in full song. You are fully embodied, fully ALIVE, fully present and totally entangled with love. You are in the moment, conscious, awake and most of all – YOU ARE HOME!

It took me a long time to come "home." I never fully inhabited my body. I essentially spent much of my life "homeless!" At the minimum, I felt as if I was renting the body I had whilst I waited for a better body to come along. I greedily eyed up other bodies that I deemed to have it all and fantasised that if I had *that* body I would feel wonderful. If I had her arms, her hips, her flat stomach and her endless legs I would have no problems in the world! I would feel safe, loved, valued, cherished and cared about. Sadly the only time I really felt safe was when I disappeared into a bowl of ice cream or drowned myself in a vat of tomato ketchup and chips!

My relationship with me was about as destructive and toxic as you can get. I did everything I could to try and bully my body into the shape I desired and craved. I remember standing in front of a mirror at a health farm. I had lost a lot of weight. I was as slim as I could be but although I had physically changed my body, my relationship with me was like it had always been – harsh, critical, not feeling good enough and demanding that I conform to unrealistic ideas of perfection! Whilst my body was slim, my head was still locked in my old mindset of feeling fat and ugly and I simply couldn't see me! This was a turning point in my life as I realised that my body wasn't the issue. It was my *relationship* with my body that needed to change. Whilst I was engaged in a full on war with my body, I could never experience the abundance and joy of life. For every critical thought I had, a thousand happy ones disappeared. There is a saying that we are not a body with a soul but a soul with a body! I resonated with this. My soul desperately wanted to run free and express my deepest longings. But my mind was my jail and my feelings about my body were the bars that held me captive.

However, my body in its wisdom kept bringing me back to the same place. No matter how much weight I lost or gained I kept coming back to the same old crossroads in my life with the same old worn out questions. "Will you choose love or fear? Will you be authentic or live a life that isn't yours? Will you love me or abandon me?" Will you listen to your souls calling and create your dreams? Will you fall in love with me? My body brought me the messages my soul so desperately needed me to hear.

The call of the body

Eventually I began to listen. When Arthritis crept into my bones and inflammation flared through my flesh I began to take notice. When the discs in my back said, "Too much – no more, we cannot support you!" I stopped in my tracks. When little hard stones of pain had to be removed from my gall bladder I wondered what I was creating? When my physical pain became too great, I began to ask my body, "What is it you want? What do you need to say? What have you been trying to tell me?" Finally, I began to really start to listen to my body. Although the clues were always there in my journals that I had written over the years. Reading back on them they were always so full of my demands, my wants, my disappointments with my body. Not a day went by without a comment on how I looked, what weight I was, how much I still had to lose. Every Monday I started a new diet, every day I listed how many calories I had eaten, how much exercise I had done. My life looked more like a mathematical equation than a joyful experience! And underneath my demanding words was a subtext that I never paid attention to. The voice of my body trying so hard to tell me what I most needed to hear. In a major turn around I wondered what it would be like to let my body write a journal. I was curious about what my body had to say. Maybe it knew better than my mind, which had been wrapped up in old conditioning from the past. Maybe the happiness I had always longed to find was right here already within my body.

And so, I decided to hand the pen over and keep a diary written from my body. I decided that I would write my journals from the perspective of my body rather than my critical and judgmental mind. I wondered what kind of a body story my own body would write if it had the chance. The results amazed and humbled me.

Body Dialogue

My body's voice astounded me. It was always loving, always forgiving and always on my side. No matter what I had inflicted upon my body I was aware of a deep unconditional love that had always been there and always would be. My body reassured me it was okay. It soothed me and whispered to me when I was despairing of ever changing. Every page began with recognition of how I felt and how much my body was doing to help me feel better. Every page ended with some kind words..."You're doing so well, keep going, you'll get through this, I'm with you, I LOVE YOU"

I began to have a new perspective about how I looked at my body. When the people I loved most in my life died, my heart broke but mended stronger than before...laced together with the memories of their love. When crippled with arthritis and in bed for six months my legs learned how to walk and dance again. When too much food and too much alcohol left me sick in bed, my body forgave me. No matter how tired I was my body got me out of bed to face another day. And at night when I tumbled into a restless sleep my body kept on working, protecting me, loving me and seeing me gently through my darkest hours.

I was so amazed by the eternal grace and love of my body. Whilst other people may have walked away from me, my body never failed me, never forgot me, and never lost sight of where I (my soul and essence) truly lived. I am overwhelmed by how much my body has always loved me even when I had hated it with a vengeance. How could I *not* love my body when it did so much for me? I realised that I had only ever looked at my physical shape and had never noticed the shape of my beautiful soul; a shape that my body now dances with joyously and playfully. Sometimes it's a dramatic tango as life calls us to kick up our heels. Other times it's a slow passionate waltz as I embrace my soul gently and tenderly. Sometimes we just walk out together on a summer's day and delight in the fact that we can. The hunger I now feel is an insatiable appetite and desire for life. I believe this has always been there...from the six-year-old ballet dancer who was told, "You are too fat to dance!" To the adult woman who believed she was too broken to be loved. Underneath my entire life's journey the whispers of my soul were kept safe within my body until I could listen without running and feel without doubting. I am so privileged, humbled and blessed to have this body – MY body. What other relationship gives you so much? Who else will stand for you, keep your dreams alive, heal you, nurture you, believe in you and be with you right to the end, when this particular physical journey is over.

Body "Post its!"

Inspired by writing my body journal I began to write little notes back to my body. These always began with the words, "Dear body, today I promise you that I will...."

My body had given so much to me that I wanted to give a little back to my body. The promises I made were easy, kind and doable. Gone were the days of declaring I would lose a stone in a month. Instead I gently promised that I would drink a bit more water or go to bed earlier. I promised that I would be more attentive and aware of my feelings. I promised I would slow down a little and take time to reflect. I promised not to say Yes, unless it was a wholehearted yes. I promised I would be kinder, more patient and more compassionate. And when my body was in pain, instead of being angry and frustrated that I couldn't do what I wanted to do, I spent time soothing the area that hurt. I wrote these little promises on "post it" notes, which I read every day. I put them around my house. I opened the kitchen cupboard and a note would fall out reminding me of my promise to feed my body what it truly loved! I hid these notes everywhere...in my underwear drawer, my handbag, my car, my mirror, my shoes, my makeup bag, my purse, my diary. Endless little promises that I would "forget" that I had written and then be surprised when I opened the cake tin and found a note saying that I promised my body a hug before I had a cake! It made me laugh. It interrupted my old way of thinking. It was so simple and yet so soul-full.

I began to tune in to what my body was saying on a daily basis. I was listening. Something was happening. Something was changing. At times, songs would fall around me and wrap me up in their melody. Goosebumps would rise and fall on my arms as I touched the truth of my being. Sometimes rushes of pure energy and excitement would flood through me opening me up to the possibility of my life. I felt alive. I was smiling. I was co-creating with my body and I loved it. We had become partners. My body spoke and I simply took dictation! (What a turn around from how it had been in the past!). I was re-connecting and listening to the whispers within and slowly and rather wonderfully "Romancing your body" was born.

Write your own Body Diaries (Body Love Coaching Exercise)

One beautiful way to begin to reconnect and get to know your own body's voice is to write your own body journal or diary. Many people have enjoyed the benefits of writing a gratitude journal as a way to deepen their own connection with the Universe and feeling good. Writing to your body takes this practice one step further. Not only does this exercise help you tap into those heartfelt emotions of wellness and health but it is a powerful and effective way of deepening and forging your relationship with your own body. Buy yourself a note book and on the left hand side of the page, write down whatever you are grateful to your body for. Begin by writing the heading "Dear Body, Today, I am grateful for..." Write down at least three things that you are thankful to your body for. This might be something that you have experienced during the day that your body has done for you. Maybe you have managed to feel less tired, or perhaps that head cold has now gone. You might want to write about what your body has allowed you to experience today; the hug of a loved one, laughter, seeing a beautiful sunset or listening to your favourite uplifting music. It's easy to find things to thank your body for. You are alive, you are here. There is another chance for you to heal, grow and move past your old limitations. Thank your body for another breath, another taste of life, for digesting your food, for walking, dancing, singing, reading, writing or just being able to communicate with the people you meet. Aim to write at least three things that you feel grateful to your body for.

Then on the right hand side of the page, write a message from your body back to you. Pretend that you are your body and are speaking from your body's point of view. Stand back a little and take time to imagine what it would be like if your body could speak and what it might want to say. The easiest way to do this is to think of three positive caring qualities that you have observed yourself do today. These might be that you drank more water, allowed yourself to relax a little more. Maybe you moved more or took time to go out for a walk. The smallest things count here and they matter. It's often much harder writing from your body's perspective, simply because we seldom take time to see it. It's not something that most of us are familiar or comfortable with. Many people have never even thought of writing a letter or a note from their body so just doing this can feel odd or uncomfortable. I would implore you to stay with this. It's such a powerful tool and technique to help you really begin to shift your perception about your body. This is where the relationship with you and your body can really begin to heal as you take time to "talk" to each other. You may have to dig deep. It's easy to dismiss the things we have done because they weren't perfect in some way. For example, you may feel that you ate too much or drank more than you wanted to. Just being aware of this is a positive quality. Write it down as if your body has observed this in you. An example of what your body's message may go something like this;

Dear (insert your own name), What I love most about you today is the way you kept trying to do the best for me. Thank you for being aware that you had eaten too much and that I felt uncomfortable. Thank you for doing this journal and trying to connect with me. Just being able to step out of your usual self identification of what it's like to be you and view yourself from your body's perspective is a powerful shift in consciousness. So often it's hard to see anything positive that we do for our body.

We are usually so wrapped up in judging or criticising ourselves and our body that we fail to see all of the positive qualities that we have. Even so called negative or self punishing behaviour can be viewed in a positive way. For example, I used to be really tough on my body when it came to exercise. I disliked my body so much that I used the gym or workouts as a way to punish and whip my body into shape. I would spend hours in the gym hoping to sweat off a few pounds and felt disappointed if I didn't manage to achieve this. When I wrote my own body gratitude journal I found it really difficult to write anything positive from my body's point of view about the way I exercised. It was harsh and unforgiving. I often went on exercising far too long and ignored the signs of fatigue that my body was giving me. However, I eventually managed to pull out the positive intentions behind how I treated my body. My body wrote the following:

" Dearest Astrid, I can see that you are really trying to make some changes with me. I know that your intentions are good. Maybe you could treat me a little gentler – I think I would be able to respond more as I would be less tired. I do enjoy all the dancing though – that makes me feel wonderful. Maybe we can do more of that? You have amazing determination and I can see that you want to feel good about me."

The key is to make a caring connection. Without connection we have no communication. Without care we have no purpose. Writing the body gratitude journal is a wonderful way to really forge the relationship between you and your body. When it comes to your body, most people have little or no relationship with it. Even calling your body an "it" strikes me as remarkably detached and removed. Maybe we can find a better terminology than "it." Perhaps you could call your body "her" (or "him" if you are a guy reading this). Maybe we don't even need to give our body a gender based name. Perhaps all that is needed is a loving adjective before the word body such as beautiful, beloved, gorgeous, sweet, amazing or fabulous! The point is that however you decide to refer to your body, do it with love, respect, kindness and an awareness of how incredible your body truly is. The poet Mary Oliver has a lovely turn of phrase for the body which she describes so eloquently in her poem The Wild Geese. This paragraph is taken from the poem;

> *"You do not have to be good.*
> *You do not have to walk on your knees*
> *for a hundred miles through the desert, repenting.*
> *You only have to let the soft animal of your body*
> *love what it loves.*

How beautiful. You only have to let the soft animal of your body loves what it loves. When I think of my own beloved pets and their beauty and softness, I find myself relating also to the soft animal of my *own* body. She desires love, attention, to be held and whispered to, to be fed and moved and to rest and sleep in the safety of a haven of acceptance and care in her forever home.

A sacred romance – a spiritual journey

For me, the greatest romance is the soul's love affair with the body and the most spiritual and loving thing that I can do is to be a channel for all of that love to come pouring through me. I can then give freely and openly to others in my life. It's interesting as sometimes "Spiritual awakening" is frequently described as a journey to the top of a mountain, whereby we focus on leaving our attachments to the world behind as we slowly make our way to the top. Once ascended we are free! However, I see spiritual awakening more as a journey that goes in and down into the very core and depths of our being. Instead of moving away from turbulence, fear and doubt I seek to welcome it and embrace its message. Instead of dancing around it or tiptoeing quietly around its volcanic jagged edges I now jump into the very middle of its fiery core and question what it wants from me and how I can be with it rather than trying to escape. When we allow life and experiences to be as they are without judgment, opinion, criticism or demanding that they be any other than what is present we move down and in to the very stillness and acceptance of our authentic self. Right in the core of our own beautiful being we discover the eternal nugget and lodestone of truth that has always been there. Right in the middle of all of the chaos, frustration, anger and despair we discover the love that will never die. The love that can only be experienced by standing within your own immense light and choosing to shine no matter what and in any way that you can! Like the proudest tallest lighthouse in the Universe we continue to radiate out streams of conscious sparkles of light that illuminate the way for many another traveller.

Loving your body is a sacred act. It's more than simply liking the shape of your nose or the contours of your hips. It's about honouring the very soul and essence of you that lives within each and every cell. We often think of our body only in terms of the vehicle that transports us through our daily life. Sometimes that journey is smooth, other times it's a bumpy ride. We judge our body on whether they are behaving or functioning in the way we want and condemn them when they're not. However, your body and soul are not separate. You are an embodied being. What your soul experiences, your body experiences and vice versa. Everything is energy and information. Every single part of your body carries within her flesh the wisdom of the Universe and the DNA of time itself. When you begin to view your body in this sacred and holistic (almost holographic way) then you begin to see yourself differently. When you consider that every part of your body is your soul in physical form expressing its own story and wisdom, your perception changes radically. No longer are you just stuck in your head or wandering about with a soul floating somewhere outside of your body – you are "home"

My soul is fat!

When I truly "got" this, my body became the focal point of how I brought *more* of my soul into being. Instead of holding back thinking that I couldn't step out into the world because I was too big, too old or any of the other fears I had, I asked myself different questions. These were as follows:

- What is the gift that I am here to share?
- What is the message I am here to give?
- What do I desire to feel every day of my life?
- How can I honour the calling of my soul within my body?
- What is it my soul most wants to experience within my body?

I realised that my soul was huge! It was enormous in its appetite for life, love, experiences and creativity. Every new diet with all of its restrictions also starved my soul for what it really desired. Every time I reigned myself in or turned away from what I *could* be, my soul withered a little more. But the truth is that my soul is fat and it desires to be gloriously huge! It is brimming over with hundreds of books that I have in my heart to write and it has space for more! It is full of yearning for the experiences that life and being ALIVE has to offer. It seeks to see the beauty and excitement it feels reflected back in the sweet embrace of my physical body. My soul longs to dance, to move, to laugh to create and to connect with other beautiful fabulous souls who are all so full of their own wild, passionate living. More than anything else, my soul craves to be loved with a passion that lights up the deepest reaches of space. This is what I am here for. To live and love deeply, irrevocably and fearlessly! The questions I asked myself shifted my outlook about what I was truly here to experience, create, be and do. I knew without a shadow of a doubt that it wasn't about losing weight or having tightly toned arms or any of the other things I had strived so hard to get. I knew that it was all about how much *love* I could feel and share with others every moment of my life. I understood that every single thing I thought, spoke, ate, created and experienced mattered because it was about expressing the vastness of my soul! I understood that it was about getting IN to my body instead of doing everything I could to escape. And, as someone who had spent the greatest part of my life trying to get away from my body, my hugest gift, learning and joy has been in being able to accept and love ALL of me and not run for the hills or the fridge in order to escape.

Let's make a choice to become more fully alive and plugged in to the greatest experience of what it means to be ourselves. Let's make a conscious decision to befriend us, love us, cherish us, listen to us and celebrate who we are every moment of every day so that we can live empowered fabulous magnificent, messy, glorious and wonderful lives! Let's declare to the soft breezes of the night and the warming winds of the day that we are ready to be enchanted by our hearts, gathered by our own body's wisdom and swept off our feet time and time again as we fall into the gentle caress of our own loving arms.

Power Body Relationship Coaching Question

Stop reading. Grab a notebook and pen and spend a few moments to really allow yourself to answer these questions.

- What would it feel like to really inhabit your body?
- What would it be like to love every single part of your body and infuse her with love?
- What difference might this make – mentally, emotionally, physically and spiritually?
- What does your body need in order to heal, feel good and in harmony?

- Where do you repeatedly leave your body? (when do you "forget" to love and look after you or talk unkindly about your body?
- Who are you becoming?
- What are you resisting?
- What is the lie you keep telling yourself?
- How have you withheld yourself from life?
- What does your body most need from you?

3

ROMANCE YOUR BODY WITH ACCEPTANCE!

The Soul Body Promises

I remember coaching a beautiful young girl and watched as she stared into the mirror at her face and then down at her body. It was as if she was seeing her self for the first time but it was clear that she had met her body and her appearance many times before. As she looked she seemed to be searching for something that she couldn't find in the cold glass image of her reflection. She pulled at her cheeks and looked deeply into her eyes; searching. She ran her hands down the sides of her body grimacing as she came across her stomach and her hips. There wasn't a kind word to be said about her body. She proceeded to dissect the different parts of her body. I asked her what she saw. She began with her overall look – 17 stone of fat. This set the scene for the rest of her story. The rest of the body chapters unfolded. She held up her arms and judged them harshly as padded wads of embarrassment. She could barely look at her stomach.

"I hate my stomach," she pronounced. "It's the worst thing about me!"

Her legs didn't fare much better.

"Thunder thighs," she declared with no emotion in her voice. She was simply stating a fact.

She turned slightly, sighed as her hands pointed at what she described as her enormous bottom. Turning back to the mirror she took her whole body in as her hands flickered up to her bust. She looked down and simply dismissed her breasts as being too small and too droopy. Nothing about her body seemed to fit her life. Nothing about her body gave her pleasure or joy. She told me that she didn't let anyone see her body. She told me she'd had enough.

I asked, "Is there any part of your body that you like?"

She thought for a moment and said, "I guess my ears are okay." She stumbled over her words as she said, "How sad, that the only things remotely acceptable about me are my ears..."

"How does your body make you feel?" I asked quietly, watching as she winced slightly before answering. A pause, another long sigh before the answer that was patently obvious.

"Sad, angry, frustrated!" she said in almost a whisper.

I could see tears welling up as she tried to stem the emotions that were threatening to overwhelm her.

"I wish I was slim." I wish I had a different body. If I had a different body, I'd be happy!"

Caught up in her emotions she turned to me and said, "The me inside this body is different. I'm not the person you see on the outside. I wish people could see the *real* me. Somewhere underneath all of the layers of this fat is the real me. I need to lose weight so that you can see the real me." I asked her what the real her was like. She smiled slightly and her eyes lit up for a split second. "The real me is light, happy, full of energy, flowing and not scared to take risks or follow my dream. The real me laughs easily and isn't worried by what other people think or say. The real me is FREE!" She looked lighter somehow after just saying these words. It's interesting as what she was describing were *feel-*

ings not body parts or how her body had to look. In fact there wasn't a mention of her body in her description of what the *real* "her" was like. She didn't say the real me has a flat stomach or skinny thighs. She was describing how she wanted to FEEL and believed that her body shape and appearance stopped her from feeling light, happy, flowing and free. However in truth, her body is the doorway to accessing these feelings and everything that she desires to experience in her life.

Like so many people she blamed her body for not being light, free, happy and full of energy. She believed in the old body paradigm that in order to feel fabulous you have to change the shape or appearance of your body first...then fabulosity will naturally follow. However it's the wrong way around! You can change your body to become the slimmest most honed, toned and sleekest version of you, but if you haven't learned to truly love your body and really take care of you along the way those magical light and joyful feelings will always evade and avoid you!

Whenever I ask my clients why they desire to change their body in some way their answers always describe how they want to *feel!* I believe what they are really talking about is their soul – the part of us that we have always known or intuited is the "real" us. The part that we feel more kinship with than the body we see reflected back to us in the mirror. The ultimate truth and knowing of whom we all authentically are.

How many of us have experienced similar feelings? That within us we are aware of a vibrant eternal life force – a feeling so fabulous that it's hard to define. This is the innermost feeling of our true nature – our souls calling to run wild and free amidst the landscape of our untethered and wondrous lives. A feeling and an energy so powerful and so vast that it seems that we almost could not contain all of that humungous living in a body such as ours!

We deem ourselves unworthy of such a multitude of living, greatness, brilliance and joy. We question ourselves; who am I to feel so uplifted, energised and buoyant when so many others are starving, in pain or lead lives of discontent? As the author Marianne Williamson says, Who are you *not* to? And so we try to shut down this indomitable life force and spirit in many ways, excess food being just one of them. We go on diets or restrict how much we eat. We try endlessly to make our outer body fit the shape of our soul. But it's impossible; it's the wrong way around. It can never be done for the outer body will never resemble the wisp of a willow, a starlight feather, a taffeta kiss, a gossamer dream or butterfly whispers on a summer's night. Our bodies can never be thin enough to slip through the secret fantasies of our lives. They can never be small enough to be lifted up in one hand and placed delicately in the most exquisite jewellery box, which is kept, cherished and worn with pride.

This is not the territory of the body – this is the landscape of the soul. And so instead of starving or punishing our beautiful bodies we have to learn how to feed our magnificent souls instead. We have to feed them more of what it is they truly hunger for. As long as all of our focus and attention is placed upon trying to force the body to comply with external images, should's, and trying to fit into a limited body belief we will always be out of step with the dance of our soul. We have to view our body through the eyes of the soul, not just our physical eyes. Why? Because the eyes of the soul will always tell you the absolute truth of whom you really are. The eyes of your soul will see and affirm your beauty and uniqueness to you in every moment. The soul doesn't need a mirror to know that you are and always will be eternally fabulous, gorgeous and completely adored and lovable. When you look at your reflection in the mirror only with your physical eyes it's as if you are only allowing yourself to see one side of you. It doesn't tell the *full* story of who you truly are. It's similar to stepping on the scales and judging yourself by your weight. The scales only tell you a number. They don't tell you the countless times you've overcome great obstacles and challenges in your life. They can never speak of how talented, creative and loving you are. They have no idea of your life's lessons or how much joy you have brought to others just by being you. No, the scales can only tell you a number, which changes constantly throughout the day. So when you look in the mirror make sure that you look deeply and linger awhile so that your soul can be seen fully. It takes a few moments to allow your soul to shine through because it has to get through the mind's judgements and criticisms, the memories of not being good enough or a lifetime of being compared to your older sister, best friend or the skinny models in the magazines. But if you stay awhile and are prepared to give yourself some time and love, something rather wonderful begins to happen. Your eyes begin to adjust from the mind fog of the past and as the mists of time clear away you begin to see your authentic self. It's a brave, courageous act of self-love to linger this long with only your reflection and your awesome soul. I have known many women (and men) turn away from the mirror in utter disgust and shame at what they see. It's as if I have asked them to do the worst thing in the world as I invite them to meet themselves and say "hello" to who they truly are.

Imagine yourself in a new relationship with someone you have just met and want to get to know better. Would you continually look away in disgust? Would you try to avoid being with them and really seeing them for who they are? Would you judge and condemn them without getting to know a little more about their dreams, their life, their aspirations and personal story? If you did, there wouldn't be a relationship.

It's the same with learning to romance your body and fall in love with your life. The first step and the greatest promise you can ever make yourself is to accept YOU! ALL OF YOU! This begins with becoming curious about you.

It's about being willing to see yourself in new ways with new eyes – the eyes of your soul. It means making a conscious decision to close the book of your old body story and start searching for a new brand new, real and fabulous story about the truth of YOU! This time, instead of choosing a fictional novel about your body and your life, you decide to go straight for non-fiction! Now, it's easy – you can cut away the body drama, the old beliefs and fantasies that had you bound to its glittering golden pages but left you withered in return. Now, you can open up new sacred fresh pages on which you can write your own story – your own beautiful narrative about what you desire to feel in your life and who you truly are! To begin this story, like any story, you have to start with where you are. It means first and foremost in honouring your life journey up to this point. It means looking at yourself with wonder instead of judgement and finding yourself and your body irresistible. There is no other way your romance can begin. Your mind may try to convince you that you still need to lose weight or change some aspect of your body in order to be valued or loved but you know this is fiction! It always has been. Think of one of your best friends or someone you love very dearly in your life. Do you love them for the shape of their body or the way they look? Or, do you love them because they are who they are and the joy and love they bring to your life? When they say they look too fat, old or tired, do you nod your head and agree with every word? Or, do you point out every wonderful thing about them that you can find? We seek to uplift and nurture the people we love. We try to reflect back the wonder and beauty that we see in them so that they might see it for themselves.

The gift you bring others is the present you need to bring to yourself. It's not a hard thing to do – you've already done it thousands of times before in your life. You know how to point out the positive attributes of another person. You know how to be kind. You are already a skilled master at uplifting someone else's spirits. This isn't something new that you've got to learn. The only thing you need to change is the direction of the love. As well as giving it out to someone else, start to give it back to you too!

We don't treat others as we treat ourselves. We don't see others as we see ourselves.

Cut out the wiggle room!

You can't wiggle around this one. You can't *pretend* to accept you – it will never work. You can't make excuses, avoid, escape, deny, reject or run away anymore. Who are you running from? You (the authentic you) is always there, just waiting patiently for you to see that the greatest romance of all time is just waiting for you to discover it! In any case I am sure that, like me you have tried the escape route many times before and it simply doesn't work. You would think that we would cop on and realise that the things we have been doing has never yielded the results we were looking for. However, such is the grand illusion and delusion of fairytales that we keep on repeating the same things in the random hope of a different outcome.

This is the tantalising allure of the fictional story. We keep believing that we will be saved and rescued by some glorious being who we will fall in love with forever. What we fail to understand is that this glorious being is us! We really *are* the one we have been seeking all of our life! Many of us have been brought up to believe that we will only find this kind of divine love in the heart of another. And so we keep seeking in the nooks and crannies outside of our body, our energy and our truth. We try to change our shape to match the ideal form of another's fantasy or the latest look of the day. We cram and stuff down our innermost dreams, feelings, longings and callings in order to embody the beige coloured shape of mediocrity. And all of the time our own heart sings in glorious technicolour and whispers to us longing to be heard, to be felt and to be treasured for the love and wisdom it holds. We try to live in accordance with someone else's rules. We minimise and subdue our preferences in order to maximise and elevate someone else's.

We are constantly being shaped and reshaped by the influences in the external world and environment around us. Everything that we hear, see, read, touch, smell, and encounter is shaping our experience of who we are in relation to what we are coming into contact with. We are shaped by everything in our external and also internal environment. The only way to break free from this subtle (and sometimes not so subtle) conditioning is to actively choose a different path, perspective, purpose and passion. This means that you begin by accepting everything about you right now. It means that you meet yourself exactly where you are – in this moment. It also invites you to recognise everything in your life that has happened to bring you to this exact point in time and to accept it as if you had chosen it. (Which, on a deeper level – you have). When you accept everything about you right now – just as you are without judgement, negative thoughts, harsh criticisms or feeling ashamed, you embark on one of the greatest romances and relationships of all time. The one with YOU!

Hating or fighting with yourself doesn't work on any level. It will never create the joy, peace, happiness or freedom you desire – it will only create more stress. We are taught to fight our so-called imperfections. The old body paradigm and body culture made it acceptable to fight our bodies or complain about our shape, our weight, our wrinkles etc. It made it acceptable for people's bodies to be paraded in magazines with negative, unkind and cruel comments hurled at the photo. And in judging the body of another we also bought into the erroneous belief that it was okay to also judge our own.

The inner peace of acceptance

If you really want to change a habit, or a situation, or how you feel about yourself, the only route that will bring you any peace is to start with acceptance. From here you can make an informed decision about whether change is even necessary in the first place. Whenever you don't accept yourself you never truly HAVE yourself. In non-acceptance we keep ourselves miles away from the person we most desire to be. The problem with this is that nothing can ever change, develop or grow because we're not really there. You don't ever HAVE you and as such if you never HAVE you, how can you change anything about you? Acceptance also means that you embrace the way that you *feel* in the moment. So often we try to hide, deny or disown the feelings that we find uncomfortable or we try to suppress our anger or frustration. However, in doing this we are actually binding and locking these feelings more deeply into our body. It takes a huge amount of energy to constantly be in a state of protection, projection, rejection or avoidance with ourself. We may try to ignore an issue but our body knows it's there – it can FEEL it. There is a saying that goes "our issues are in our tissues" This is so true as our body simply seeks to obey and manifest our thoughts, beliefs, perceptions and opinions about who we are and our relationship with the world. Every cell in your body feels your thoughts and processes them chemically.

Begin to open your body, mind and heart into accepting and embracing ALL of you by allowing *all* of your feelings to be present – not just the "good" ones! This doesn't mean that you wallow in the sad, negative or angry feeling but that you observe that the feeling is there without becoming attached to it or hooked into it! Instead of judging the feeling, you welcome it in – you turn to face it and be with it rather than run from what you fear or avoid. When you are able to allow the feeling to be present with a loving and caring response from YOU, your entire relationship changes! Rather than being consumed by the negative emotion or feeling, you are able to be there with it and befriend it and then let it go. It is said that an emotion only takes around ninety seconds to pass through our bodies; to be felt and expressed. However, when we block our feelings or deny our emotions we hold on to them for far longer than ninety seconds. I held on to my own anger and frustration for years by continually blaming my body for causing me so much unhappiness and grief! Instead of feeling what I felt and addressing it in the moment, I shut the feeling down in any way I could. I denied what I felt or I ate what I felt. If someone asked me how I was feeling I would reply with my standard response of "fine!" Even if I was feeling anything *but* fine! I remember being told once in my coaching and counselling training what "fine" actually stood for. It was Freaked, Insecure, Neurotic and Emotional! That pretty much summed me up! Accepting your feelings means allowing yourself to actually feel them and be open to the wisdom, insight and healing they bring. "*You have to feel if you want to heal*" is an expression I carry with me today which reminds me to be present for all of me! The key is to *feel* the feeling and then let it go – allow it to move through all of your body, mind and soul.

Body Acceptance Coaching Exercise

Just stop right where you are and take a deep full breath. What are you feeling right now? How are you feeling right now? What are you aware of? Can you name this feeling, what is it? If it's difficult to find a name for it or the feeling feels too vague, tap into how your energy is right now. Is it high and buoyant, or low, slow and lethargic? Do you feel open and expansive or contracted and closed down? Whatever you may or may not be feeling, say out loud, "I completely accept how I'm feeling right now". Stay curious and inquisitive about what you feel without any judgement or criticism. There is no right or wrong way to feel, only the way that you are feeling in the moment.

Repeat this exercise from time to time during your day. Just pause and come back to you and check in with how you are feeling and accept whatever is there with kindness and compassion.

Life is good

Life is good. It's a fundamental truth. No matter what – life is good. Whilst we are alive we have the chance to change to do something good, no matter how small and insignificant. We have the chance to smile at another human being. We have the opportunity to breathe in and breathe out love. However, when you are at war with your body or not treating yourself kindly, life doesn't feel good. It's a struggle and each day becomes something to be got through rather than enjoyed and actively participated in.

And yet, life is good.

For many years I could not see that life was good; that **I** was good. That good could come from bad situations. That the worst that could happen probably already had. So I ate. I ate to keep my feelings down and my life force low. I ate to take fear as my prisoner and trap it forever in my fat cells. "You can't get out now – I've got you! I hope you suffer." And suffer it did but then, so did I. I ate to dim my lights and bury my dreams. I ate to put a lid on my energy and fill in the moments of endless nothing. I took in more than my body could ever want. I loaded myself down with the kind of calories that take your life away. I ate to stop time. I ate to disconnect myself from a world I felt was too harsh and unforgiving. I ate because.... I just ate. Eating was a way I communicated with myself and with the world. When I was eating I was talking. However, most of my conversation merely said the one thing over and over again.

"I am afraid."

"Afraid of what?"

It didn't matter. I was simply afraid. Being fearful was written across my heart and coursed its message throughout my body. If you had cut me open, you would have seen the words "fear" running through my core. Rather like a stick of rock, fear was imprinted on my soul and ran deep within my veins. But fear is one of the most powerful allies we've got. Fear alerts you to where your deepest truths lie and your most authentic life awaits. Fear heralds the need to change. In emergencies fear is our motivator – it calls us to take action. Whether it's to stand still or run, we feel the adrenalin of fear and we respond accordingly. And when the fear is made up of our doubts and insecurities, our worries or our learned beliefs, fear calls us to question the untruths that we live by. Fear challenges us in the hopes that it can change us. Change happens when you confront the fear; when you stand your ground and turn your face to your reflection in the mirror and say, "Is this true?"

"Is it true that I'm not good enough?"

"Is it true that I can't cope on my own?"

"Is it true that I'm not able to manage my feelings?"

"Is it true that I am powerless to live the life I dream about?"

"Is it true my body needs to be "perfect" before I can love it?"

"Is it true that I can't love me?"

"Is it true that I will always eat compulsively and mindlessly?"

And to all of those questions the answer is "NO"

None of those beliefs were true...they were just big fat lies that I told myself day after day, year after year and I chose to believe them as if they were my bible. To change anything you have to stop feeding yourself big fat lies. They neither nourish nor nurture you. All they do is fill you full of fear.

What will you eat? Fear or love?

What will you believe? Fearful thoughts or loving thoughts?

What will you talk about? What you want or what you don't want?

And so today I live by choosing to love. To love me, my life, others, the world and even fear itself. I am grateful to my fears; they showed me how to love and go deeper than I have gone before. If I had never experienced what fear can achieve I could never have felt what love has to bring. The greatest gift is being able to live WITH fear rather than IN fear. I listen to my fears and instead of believing them I am alert to them. I am curious about what message they bring and I ask myself questions. "What's wrong? What makes me believe this? What do I need? What am I not saying? Where am I forgetting me?"

These are powerful questions and they bring me back home time and time again.

And if fear should come calling during the night I'll invite it in and sit it by the fire and give it the space it needs. I'll make a cup of tea and wrap my rug around it and ask it gently and kindly, "What brings you here, my friend? What do you need? What message do you have for me?" These days I accept that at times I will feel fearful and that it's okay. It's okay not to have all the answers. It's okay to feel afraid and vulnerable; it's okay not to have to be in constant control. This kind of acceptance has allowed me to drop the struggle in my life and with my body. In accepting and allowing myself to be exactly as I am, I allow others to be exactly who they are and how they are too. It's a glorious feeling – full of peace and kindness. It softens and opens my heart to the entire experience of life and I find myself falling more in love with the world with all of its beauty and frailties!

I'm so sorry you hurt

Accepting and loving our body can be one of the most challenging journey's we ever make. I know from my own personal body experience how hard it can be to accept your body. In the past I would have done everything that I could to avoid meeting me in the mirror. I didn't like me, I didn't want to be in the body I had. I resented and rejected my body and it didn't matter what I did to my body in order to make it comply with the ideas of "perfection" that I had in my mind. However, the body journey is always one of coming back home. Time and time again my body would bring me back to the place where I needed to take action, change and move beyond my old conditioning and body hatred. I remember one day sat in the hospital waiting room just before I was about to see my consultant for my arthritis. I felt awful. My weight was around twenty one stone and I was suffering with chronic pain in my knees, feet, fingers and neck. My blood pressure was sky high and on top of this I had constant rhinitis, which left me continually blowing my nose. It was one of the lowest times in my life. I seemed to have a permanent headache and just wanted to give up. As I left the hospital that day with a prescription for some fairly toxic medication, I decided that I had two choices. I could go on resisting and denying that I needed to take care of my body or I could simply accept where I was and be the best that I could be no matter what. It was liberating! Hurting me hadn't helped so perhaps loving me would! I decided there and then that if I was going to be a size 30 then I would be the very best size 30 I could be. Instead of resisting and feeling angry about my pain I made a choice to be compassionate towards my body. When my knees would protest and cry out in pain as I stood up I began to say, "I'm so sorry you hurt." I began to touch my neck with compassion when every fibre felt tense and stiff. I began to have a relationship with me. If this had been someone else who was suffering in this way I would have asked them if there was anything I could do. I began to ask my body what I could do to help. It was a change. A small one initially but a significant step in being able to accept me, my body and where I was in my life.

Meet yourself in the mirror of life

What would it be like to meet yourself again and again and see your reflection everywhere? What would it feel like to walk up to the mirror, smile warmly and embrace your awesome soul body? What would it feel like to look deeply into your own eyes and behold the beauty of your magnificent soul? What would it take for you to commit to your souls journey with your body as communicator, initiator and creator of all of your most innermost dreams? Your inner life (the thoughts, feelings, opinions, joys, sorrows, peace, happiness etc) will always show up on the outside. Life is lived from the inside out. We project outwards what we believe to be true on the inside. We don't see life as it is – we see life as we are! We literally become the biology of our beliefs.

The greatest romance begins with the *willingness* to fall in love. If we are not willing to meet ourselves as we are and get to know this beautiful being and body who is with us every moment of every day, then we live outside of ourselves. Forever searching for a place to call "home" and finding it in all of the wrong places.

Clarissa Pinkola Estes describes the relationship with our body beautifully in her wonderful book, "Women who run with the wolves." She says,

"Some say the soul informs the body. But what if we were to imagine for a moment that the body informs the soul, helps it adapt to mundane life, parses, translates, gives the blank page, the ink and the pen with which the soul can write upon our lives? Suppose, as in fairy tales of the shapechangers, the body is a God in its own right, a teacher, a mentor, a certified guide? Then what? Is it wise to spend a lifetime chastising this teacher who has so much to give and teach? Do we wish to spend a lifetime allowing others to detract from our bodies, judge them, find them wanting? Are we strong enough to refute the party line and listen deep, listen to the body as a powerful and holy being?"

Our body is not some sort of unchanging statue only shaped and fashioned in specific ways to suit the body culture of the time. The idea that any body could ever be considered as "wrong" or faulty in any way is an old paradigm and one which fails to see the extraordinary connection between the incredible wisdom of our bodies and the vast expanse of our souls. The body's purpose is to protect, contain, support and inspire and fire the soul or spirit within it. The body is a repository for feelings, emotions, memories, longings, desires, dreams, hopes and wishes. It propels us and compels us and fills us with feeling. It is within our body that we understand that we exist. We are HERE! Our body gives us grounding, weight, gravity and substance. If we only think of our body in terms of being able to leave it so that we can fly free and soar to the spirit then we have missed the point of being alive. It is the body that informs the soul of what it means to be fully alive. It is only through the body's experiences that the soul can find it's fullest expression.

As Clarissa Pinkola Estes, writes,

"The body is the launcher of those experiences. Without body there would be no sensations of crossing thresholds, there would be no sense of lifting, no sense of height, weightlessness. All that comes from the body. The body is the rocket launcher. In its nose capsule, the soul looks out the window into the mysterious starry night and is dazzled."

Ask yourself – Who does this belong to?

Making the promise of acceptance begins by becoming curious about you in a loving, interested way. Step back a little from the "old" you that you think you know and begin to watch and observe the things you do, the words you say, the judgements you have and the criticisms you make. Where did they all come from? Whose voice do you hear in your head when you tell yourself that you're not good enough? Do those words sound like your mother's voice? Perhaps it's a teachers voice and opinion that you are aware of? Maybe it's the magazines that you read and you've simply internalised their message as your own? What opinions do you hold that you have always simply accepted as fact? Where did they come from? Are they even true? Relationships are formed by really getting to know someone. Think back to any relationship you have ever embarked upon. We take time to listen and to evaluate what the other person is saying. We look at their values, their dreams and their behaviour in this world. We spend hours just getting to know and understand them. We unconsciously look for ways in which what they say aligns with what they do and who they are. We are always looking for signs that we can trust this person. The underlying question is always, can we allow ourselves to give our precious heart to another? Can we allow ourselves to give our precious heart to ourself?

Begin every day with the promise of acceptance and the intention of LOVE!

The romance of a new day, a fresh morning waiting to be discovered and lived out to its fullest potential. Is there any other more beautiful feeling than the soft light of day weaving its beautiful ribbons of light across your eyes and kissing your body awake? Morning edges her loving way across the land bringing light and life back to the sleepers of the night. As you open your beautiful eyes allow them to linger awhile between the spaces between night and day, the transition of what has gone and what has not yet come to pass. Be in the moment. This moment of beginning again and setting your course for the most glorious day you can imagine and desire. A day that brings you the opportunity to BE YOU in the fullest sense of all you are and all you are yet to become. It is in this sweet moment when the day has not yet etched its story upon your skin, where everything is a blank and enticing page waiting to be written by you. You – the author of your life and the fabulous creator of your personal script. What world do you desire to live in today? How much love can you give your amazing body today?

Mindful Morning Meditation - Inhabit your body!

Before you even get out of bed, take a moment to connect with how your body feels and take stock of how you are. Take a deep breath.

Run your hands down the sides of your body, across your hips and thighs, over your abdomen and up across your ribs. Sense into how your body feels with curiosity and care. Run your hand down one arm and then up again to stroke your neck. Repeat with the other hand. Touch your face lightly. Wiggle your toes, flex your feet and feel the stretch in your calf muscles. Breathe deeply and richly, taking in and accepting your body. Allow yourself to really land and BE in your beautiful body. Stretch slowly and feel the muscles, ligaments and tendons of every part of your body begin to wake up. Lengthen your spine, ease into your shoulders, drop into your pelvis and stretch your arms. How does your body feel? Take a moment to scan your body and notice if any parts of your body feel tight or constricted in any way. If they do then close your eyes and imagine a beautiful white light full of shimmering sparkles flowing from the space between your brows (your third eye). Direct this light in a powerful and loving stream of conscious awareness to any area that you feel needs more love, healing and tenderness. Imagine the area that is receiving this light as opening up and drinking in your own sweet healing. Imagine every cell dancing, bubbling up with joy that you have noticed them and smiling happily! Allow yourself to smile back. How lovely to be so connected and accepted by you. Whisper a quiet and heartfelt "thank you" to your body for keeping you safe all through the night. What other love does this for us? What other love keeps us safe and protected all through the night without ever having to be directed or asked? As we sleep our amazing body simply keeps a watchful awareness over us, adjusting our temperature, relaxing our muscles, regulating our breathing and gently beating out the hypnotic rhythm of our heart. Night after night, no matter how much we may have ignored or mistreated our body our body simply continues to take care of us as best as it can. Often without any thanks or appreciation or acknowledgment of everything it does for us. Return the love with a quiet acknowledgment and thanks for the love your body endlessly shows you, every moment of every day and night.

Begin the day slowly and sensuously

Make rushing out of bed and tumbling into another day with no time to love (or even notice) you a thing of the past. Make the beginning moments of every single day belong to YOU first. Before everyone else gets your attention, love, and care, make these moments with you non negotiable and make them precious. Make it your own personal rule that the first person you greet and extend your love and thoughts to is YOU! We wouldn't dream of ignoring the other people who are special to us in the morning. At the very least we say "hello" and say "good morning" And yet we very rarely take time to wish ourselves a wonderful day or enquire as to how we are feeling and what would make us happy. It's such a simple thing to do. It only takes a few brief moments and it is in these moments that you create the day ahead and how you desire yourself to show up in the world. And if you know that the day ahead may bring you challenges that have been causing you to respond stressfully, then place your hand gently over your heart and say quietly in your mind... "No matter what the day ahead brings, I know that I can manage any challenges with grace, integrity, confidence, love and gratitude."

Morning Body Intentions

Make your mornings some of the sweetest moments of your day. Meet yourself anew every day with love, gratitude, kindness and grace. We so often forget these dynamic windows of opportunity in our lives, as we are too intent on rushing full steam ahead into the endless list of things that have to get done, people to look after or work to be achieved. There will always be something or someone that demands your attention so make it your priority that the first person you wish a happy day to is YOU! Set your body intentions for the day. An intention is simply a wish or a desire of what you would love to have happen or a way that you choose to be. Make it your intention to love and accept your body by looking in the mirror and saying

"I am now willing to deeply love and accept my body."

Some other examples of body intentions are:

My intention is to enjoy every moment of the day ahead in my beautiful body

My intention is to check in with my body throughout the day and say "hello! How are you?"

My intention is to slow down and listen to my body more.

I intend to drink more water today and eat with love and awareness.

My intention is to speak well of my body.

My intention is to thank my body for all that it does to keep me well.

My intention is to look after my body and enjoy being me.

The intention to give

One of the most lovingly powerful intentions you can make is to give something to your body. It can be anything you feel would really show your body that you love it. Even the smallest intention to give can reap huge rewards. Your gift of giving can be as simple as smiling at your reflection in the mirror, or buying your body something to make it feel good. It could be a bunch of flowers, a delightful body lotion, a piece of jewellery or a soft scarf. Maybe your intention is to make more time to relax. Or perhaps you just want to spend more time with you. There is something very healing and loving about just stroking your own hands with love and attention.

Embody your intentions

A lovely mindful movement meditation practice is to connect your breath with your intention. Decide on something you want to embody in your life. Close your eyes and place your hands on your heart. Breathe in and say quietly in your mind, "Today I am creating..."

Breathe out and say whatever your intention is, for example, love, inner peace, kindness, acceptance, joy, vitality, healing, compassion, abundance etc. Think of this as if you are planting a seed in your consciousness.

Repeat this breathing intention meditation for as long as it feels right for you.

Send your intention out into the world with every breath you take.

A client once said to me, when I asked her to look into the mirror and say that she deeply loved and accepted her body that it was too difficult. She couldn't do it. I asked her what she found hard. She replied that she didn't love and accept her body so it felt as if she was telling a lie. She said she felt like a fraud when she said that she loved her body or that her body was beautiful. She said she thought she should stop saying that she accepted and loved her body because it wasn't true and she didn't believe it. A lifetime of being told that her body was anything but beautiful was what she believed. A life where she put herself last on the list of people to love and care about was her "reality." A world where she avoided being seen, by others and herself was what dictated the way she showed up in her own life. All of this she believed was the *real* truth about her. As she spoke her jaw tightened and her eyes welled up with tears. She said that she didn't know how to love her body or her self. She asked me how could she ever fall in love with herself and her body? She questioned, "How do you begin to fall in love with someone that you were always told was "wrong" and didn't deserve your attention let alone your love." I asked her if there were people or animals in her life that she loved. She nodded her head. She said that there were. I asked her how she showed her love for them. How did she express her love and how did they know what she felt. She smiled and answered easily. I tell them that I love them. I make time for them. I do special things to make them happy. I sometimes go out of my way to give them what they want. I listen to them. I pay attention to them. I buy them nice things. I stand up for them. I think well of them. I put them first. I'm unhappy if they're unhappy. I try to help make their dreams happen. I sit with them when they are sad and upset. I bolster them up. I tell them they can do it and that they are wonderful. I am there for them. I love them.

I smiled and replied, "Do you accept them just as they are?"

She nodded, "Of course," she said.

I continued, "Do you still accept them when they look awful or are too tired or not in a good place?"

She smiled. "Yes, absolutely!"

I smiled at her, "Well, that's how you do it. But instead of giving all of your love, care and acceptance outwards you begin to direct it inwards towards yourself. You give all of that care, acceptance and attention to you."

She took a breath and her answer came out quietly and a bit shakily.

"But isn't that incredibly selfish?"

There it was – one of the biggest untruths and destroyers of relationships of all time. That loving yourself is a selfish thing to do. This one little lie has held so many millions of people back from experiencing their most magical lives. This one tiny but incredibly dangerous belief has halted the happiness and progression of thousands of people who dreamed of shining but kept themselves in darkness. One of the greatest and most liberating answers to this question – isn't it selfish to love yourself is simply, "SO WHAT!" So what if it's selfish? Who cares if it's selfish? Who says it's selfish? Where was it ever written in the grand scheme of things that it's selfish? Really? Is it selfish to love yourself? When you really get up close and personal and challenge this belief you begin to understand that the only thing that is truly selfish is NOT loving yourself.

It is when we refuse to love ourselves that the problems happen. When we take little care or attention of our own health and happiness. When we don't like the person we are and seek to find some small morsel of approval in the eyes of others. When we are too run down and too tired to care. That's selfish. Why? Because we become a burden in our life and in the lives of others. When you are too exhausted and too unhappy to get out of bed or take another step you're not there to be able to help or care for anyone else in your life.

When you despise yourself so much that it doesn't matter how low or burned out you are, you become unable to share your gifts and unique talents in this world. All of those wonderful, glorious, magical things that you might have created by your words, your songs, your music, your ideas or the healing that might have occurred just in the warmth and love of your touch – gone! Now – if we're talking selfish in the negative sense of the word then that's selfish! Isn't the most selfish thing you can do is never to bring your most gorgeous self to the world? The world suffers when you're not in it. More than ever we so desperately need people who are fully alive and radiating out their gifts, happiness, compassion and creativity. It's inspiring when we see people who are living their best, most happiest lives. We see so much of the opposite around us, reflected in the News. People living in fear or children who are growing up with no hope. Let's be the hope and the knowledge that *we* can change and in so doing we also play our part in changing the world.

So let's embrace selfish and see it for what it really is. If it makes you feel more comfortable you can change the word selfish into self-caring. Whatever way you want to do it, let's just own the fact that it's time to love who we are, no matter what label others may wish to place on your actions. The truth is that looking after yourself is the most loving thing that you can ever do for others.

Make the promise of acceptance

Accepting you and your body is simply a choice. It doesn't matter if you don't fully believe it or even feel as if you accept your body right now. The promise of acceptance simply asks you to *choose* a new direction in your life. It asks you to acknowledge your body every morning and make a promise to tell your body you accept it. It's not hard; it's simply a choice. The more you practice awakening and connecting with your body the more you change the habits and old patterns and programmes of the past. Just do it! Make the commitment and keep the promise of acceptance. As you get better and better at keeping the promise of acceptance, allow it to extend into every moment of your day. Accept what life brings you in your day – stop fighting against what IS! This doesn't mean that you don't take action to change certain things. On the contrary! It invites you to relax and lean into your life, accept what is there and then make conscious choices about what you need to do to bring you more love, peace and balance. One of the biggest causes of stress is desiring to be somewhere other than where you are. One of the greatest gifts of inner peace is allowing your body, your life and others to be exactly as they are and accept "what is" This means that you accept your emotions, your feelings, your aches and pains with a loving and caring heart. Instead of trying to get rid of what you feel, or feel angry because you feel it, you decided instead to simply be present with ALL of YOU!

Accepting ALL of YOU

Accepting all of you means that you welcome your thoughts, your beliefs, your actions and your feelings. Nothing is off limits.

Everything about you has value, interest and the potential to teach you MORE about who you authentically are. One of the most effective ways to do this is to start observing you. Step back a little and begin to watch yourself with compassionate curiosity and interest. Whenever you feel any emotion become more aware of what that emotion is without judging or criticising it. Just be interested. Notice where you feel more energy and aliveness through your day. Observe what makes you feel energised and happy and what drains your energy or makes you feel heavy, depressed or out of kilter. Make it your mission to become really interested in you! Whenever you have any physical pain in your body, stop and be with the area that hurts. Give it your loving attention and tell the painful area that you are here. Tell your body that you are listening and present. Ask how you can help – what your body needs you to do. Tell the painful area how sorry you are that it hurts. Talk to it as if you are speaking to someone you love very dearly. Your job is not to take the pain away but simply to be present for it and with it. If you are feeling emotional pain, then the same acceptance applies. Be with your feelings and allow them full expression. Resist the urge to shut your feelings down or suppress them in any way. Every emotion is a message, every feeling is your body's way of communicating with you. All an emotion desires to do is to be expressed. Remember that an emotion will pass through your body in about ninety seconds. That's all it takes for an emotion to be truly felt at the point that it is generated. However, when we block our feelings or keep replaying them over and over again in our minds, then what should have only lasted a short amount of time becomes embedded and embodied in our tissues, neural pathways, fascia and our subconscious minds. This is how we keep pain alive and keep repeating the patterns of dis-ease that we feel. Acceptance is the number one promise that opens the doorway for all the other promises. Nothing else has such a truly transformative and life affirming benefit than truly accepting and embracing who you are – mind, body, heart and soul.

If you have tried hating your body into submission and it hasn't brought you the joy, peace, love and happiness that you seek, then maybe it's time to love and accept yourself and see what that will bring.

The body love workout (exercise)

Stand or sit in front of a mirror.

Smile!

Take a deep breath, relax your belly and repeat after me...

I deeply love and appreciate me.

In fact I think I'm rather FABULOUS!

It's a joy to be who I am and I love the feeling it gives me!

For the best results repeat morning, noon and night and in between when needed. Think of every positive loving word you say to yourself as a rep...the more reps you do, the stronger your self-love muscle becomes.

Just a note when you are practicing these exercises. If any resistance comes up as you do them this is just a sign of how strong the old programmes, past conditioning or story was. Simply notice where you resist and carry on with the exercise. This is about building new more empowering and loving beliefs.

Body love coaching exercise – Write an apology note

Saying sorry is a beautiful way to heal and mend any relationship. When we move out of our defensive or stubborn ways of thinking and acting into a more heart centered and vulnerable space we can begin to forge new connections. When it comes to your body, this is vitally important. Many of us will have had difficult, unkind and unhappy relationships with our body. You may be so used to putting your body down that you don't even notice it anymore. It has become a way of life. This body love exercise invites you to begin a healing journey and new relationship with your body, mind, heart and soul.

Take a few moments to centre yourself. Close your eyes and breathe in and out deeply and fully. Open your eyes and write an apology note to your body from your mind. Say sorry for all the times you ignored or bullied your body into doing something it didn't enjoy or feel good doing. Take a moment to apologise for any unkind names you may have called your body. Recall any situations where you allowed your body to be hurt by yourself (or others) and tell your body what you need it to know. Tell your body what you would like to happen now and that you (your mind) is interested in having a new relationship with your body. Remember that you are writing from your mind's point of view. You may use this time to ask your body any questions about how to move forward. When you have finished, read your note (or letter) through once and put it away. In a few days time, re-read the letter and this time write a reply from your body to your mind. Imagine that your body is reading these words for the first time. What does your body want to say in response? Take your time. If the words don't come easily at first, stay with it. It can feel really odd trying to talk from your body's perspective. Many people have never connected the mind with the body. I never even used to look at my body in the mirror as I couldn't bear what I saw. I stayed resolutely in my mind and simply criticised my poor body from this place of mental judgement. Out of all of the journeys that we ever take in our lives the longest journey is the seven inches from our heads into our hearts!

4

ROMANCE YOUR BODY WITH GRATITUDE!

Dear beautiful you,

Who gets you out of bed every morning?

Who rushes to your aid when you're sick and low?

Who heals your wounds?

Who mends your bones?

Who loves you more than words can possibly say?

ME - Your fabulous body!

PS I don't mean to brag or anything but sometimes even I'm over-awed by me!

With love from your modest body! xx

Promise two is the promise of gratitude. "Thank you" is a word that says it all! It is the promise to recognise, appreciate and be grateful for all of the million and one things your body does for you second by second, day after day for the duration of your life. Our bodies are extraordinary. They are always working to give us exactly what we want. No matter how much we may neglect them, our bodies always do everything in their power to keep us well. That's their job. That's what they most desire in life – to be fully, wholeheartedly and wonderfully ALIVE! When we drink too much our body works overtime to eliminate the toxins. When we cut or injure ourselves, our antibodies fly into action to help heal the wound. When we are too tired, run down or exhausted our bodies will make us stop so that we can rest, heal and recuperate. Without your body you wouldn't be here reading these words. Without your wonderful body you would have no life, no opportunities to experience joy, love and all of the emotions that life offers us to taste and delight in.

Our body is always bringing us back. Back to the place where your heart meets your soul. Back to the moments where you are faced with the choice of abandoning and rejecting your body or accepting and giving thanks for it. There is no other force quite as powerful as the call of the body as it asks you to live fully in this present moment. The body tells it like it is. How do you feel? Your body will tell you. What foods make you feel full of energy and wellness? Your body will let you know. How do you know what decision to make? It's easy – follow the whispers, nudges and little tingles, shivers and energy fluctuations of your body.

The question your body always asks is, "What will it take for you to fully embody me today?" It invites you to live the experiences of your days and *feel* every single moment of your life through your body. It's a question that says, "Can you fully bear the pain, the frustration, the sadness, the joy and wonder, the uncertainty, the tiredness, the unfolding moments of happiness, the longing, the disappointments and all of the moments in between?" The body (like any other lover) wants to know if you will stay loving it no matter what happens in your life or how you feel? It seeks to know if you will feel the fear and love it anyway. It seeks to know if your love is unconditional or if you will only love your body if it is "behaving" or doing what you want. It desires to know if you can live your days with ease, trust and a million contradictions all-jostling for supremacy within you. Will you accept and give thanks for your undeniable humanness and say

"It's okay to be me," or will you endlessly struggle and strive to become some kind of "perfect" version of yourself, forgetting that you are already living the perfect version of yourself! Your body will always bring you back to the place of knowing – the place of being. A place that you can never escape from. A place that you are invited to return to again and again. "When will you come home?" the words whisper from your cells and languish longingly and lovingly on your skin. "Are you nearly there yet?" They chuckle as they wait for you to see their awesome beauty and give thanks for their brilliance and magnificence.

Gratitude transforms & reshapes your body

Gratitude is a power word. When said genuinely, it has the power to completely transform your state of being, energy, perspective and the body that you are living in. Every time you think a thought, there is an emotion and a visual image attached to it. Every single thought launches a cascade of neuropeptides that flood the body with the "chemicals" of what your thought "feels." For example, When you are in love or feeling thankful or deeply appreciative, the hormone Oxytocin is released which helps you to feel a closer connection and bonding. When you are thinking anxious, fearful or negative thoughts, the stress hormones, Adrenaline and Cortisol are released into the body. Whatever your most consistent emotional state happens to be is also what chemical "cocktail" is shaping your physiology and biology.

We know through science that our emotions have a profound impact on the body. Prolonged sadness can lead to depression, which in turn may deplete the immune system. Recent studies have linked gratefulness with increased feelings of satisfaction, motivation, energy and feelings of being more engaged in life. People who are consistently grateful tend to be more self motivated and have stronger feelings purpose, meaning and self acceptance. This is powerful when it comes to falling in love with you, your body and your life! Just imagine what could be possible if you decided to thank your body instead of criticising or judging it! How much energy and joy could you have if you simply began saying "Thank you dear sweet body" for all of the things that you experience every day? Thank you for getting me out of bed this morning. Thank you for seeing the beautiful sunrise. Thank you for tasting the amazing lunch I had. Thank you for breathing. Thank you for laughing so much the other day. Thank you for allowing me to hold what I love. Thank you for dancing, thank you for walking. Thank you for making love. Thank you for enabling me to experience this life. Thank you for getting over that cold so quickly. Thank you for being such an amazing teacher. Thank you for being just right exactly as you are. Thank you for showing me where you hurt. Thank you for all the endless things you do for me day after day, moment by moment. The list is endless and so is the amount of joy and vitality you can feel! Most people have no idea how good their body could feel if only they would allow it! The wonderful thing is that feeling amazing doesn't depend on anything outside of yourself for this to happen. It's not about waiting for that perfect moment when all of your stars line up and you're launched into your most heavenly life! It's about choosing to give thanks for the stars that are already there and loving the constellation of "NOW!" No matter what happens in your life, you always have a choice! People often say that they feel as if they don't have a choice when situations happen that they can't control. It's not true! You ALWAYS have a choice in the thoughts that you choose and therefore the feelings that you embody! So choose gratitude! Choose it every single moment of your incredible life and watch how deeply and passionately your body (and your life) loves you in return. When you look in the mirror see your body with the deepest appreciation for all that it does for you. See the many miles your legs have walked and how they have held you up and supported you in your life. See your beautiful belly and marvel at the eternal wisdom stored in the gentle roundness of your shape. Look at your wonderful arms and give thanks for all that they have carried in your life. Look deeply into your eyes and appreciate all the beauty you have been privileged to see in this world. Really look at your magnificent body and see it – really see it! This can be an emotional experience because we have been so used to looking at our precious body with the eyes of the harshest critic. Sometimes the toughest challenge of an entire lifetime is to be able to look deeply, lovingly and compassionately into our own eyes and behold the beauty, wisdom and eternal magnificence reflected back to us. When you can find no beauty in your body, it means you are using the wrong kind of eyes to truly see yourself. So look deeper and linger awhile as you truly connect with who you really are. Gaze at your hands as if you have just discovered them and wonder at all of the endless things they do for you. Refuse to compare your body to any other body in the world! This is YOUR body. It belongs to YOU during your lifetime. No one else knows how much your body does for you or the challenges that it has been through.

Reward Your Body

For just a moment, visualise that your body is your employee, and that you are its boss. It works hard every day, and it is responsible for supporting every single thing that you do, from walking to talking to clapping your hands at a concert. It is on the go twenty-four hours a day, seven days a week, and even works to move nutrients and oxygen through your system while you sleep. That's one amazing employee! Now, think about how you reward this employee. In every relationship we have, we love to feel valued, appreciated and that we are making a positive difference. However, when it comes to our body, we often treat this employee pretty badly, ignoring all the hard work it does successfully and concentrating on a tiny list of its flaws. To deepen your relationship with your body, try thanking it for all the good work that it is constantly doing. Give it a good all-over stretch, a warm bath, or even a luxurious massage. Buy your body a new outfit, or take it out for a walk in the park. If you don't believe that your body is an incredible employee, try making a list of all the incredible things your body is especially good at, like playing guitar, chopping an onion, typing at your computer, dancing your favourite dance, holding the things and people you love, sewing a garment etc. If you add just a few things every day, pretty soon you'll have hundreds of reasons to see how extraordinary your body truly is and how much it does for you! When you recognise what's great about your body, your body love and confidence will soar!

The body is so often taken for granted or seen as something to mould and shape to suit the latest fashion or fitness trend. The body is often judged, criticised and forced to comply with the will of the mind or forced to fit in with someone else's ideal of what the perfect body should be. However, the body has a mind of it's own and a wisdom that is as ancient as the birth of the first star in the cosmic dawn. Our body is the finest, most articulate "instrument" that we have. When we pay homage or give thanks to our body we connect to something that is much greater and infinite than us. Gratitude enables us to connect with something that is not only larger than ourselves but also fundamentally good, wonderful and reassuring. It opens our eyes to the miracle that is life, something to marvel at, revel in, and celebrate, rather than ignore or take for granted. Gratitude encourages and heightens life-enhancing states such as joy, tranquility, consciousness, enthusiasm, and empathy, while inhibiting painful emotions such as anxiety, heartbreak, loneliness, regret, and envy, with which it is fundamentally incompatible.

Wear your gratitude

Emotions, like any other thought, have a vibrational frequency. We *feel* our thoughts as they become the fabric of our being. When someone walks into a room and they are angry, tense, tired and upset – you can feel it. Without a single word being said, you know exactly the emotional state of that person. The energy is dense and contracted and emits at a low vibration. Equally, when someone is joyous, happy, light and free you feel that too! The energy and vibration is light, higher, open and playful. There is a sense of possibility and freedom and we are attracted to this higher frequency. We are exquisite at "reading" the energy vibrations of other people and also ourselves. However, many people are so used to experiencing continual low energy states that they become immune to any other state of being. The feeling of gratitude opens your heart and releases stress from your muscles. It frees your joints and even chronic pain may feel a little better when we are grateful. As someone who has suffered for many years with chronic and extremely painful arthritis I know the incredible difference between having the physical pain and causing myself real suffering! The more I resisted what was happening to my joints and struggled against the pain, the more I hurt. I was so angry that I had arthritis which had stopped me from moving, dancing and living my life that all of my focus was on hating my body and blaming it for what I couldn't do. However, as I began to learn to feel compassion and tenderness for my body, the pain began to move and my joints became freer.

Soften into your body – a healing gift

A beautiful gift you can give yourself is to learn how to soften into your body. Romancing your body means taking time for the relationship to develop. Imagine if your partner or a loved one was in pain and they had come to you for help. You would most probably spend time with them. You would move into a listening, quiet and receptive state of being. Your voice would probably soften and you would ask them to tell you what's wrong. You may even ask what you can do to help. Just your presence and willingness to be with them may even change how they feel entirely. The key is to do this with your *own* body. Whenever we reject any part of our body, we cause that area to feel separate from us. We may talk negatively about it or completely ignore it altogether. One of the most powerful and deeply transformative ways that we can truly heal our relationship with our body is to open up a gentle communication and conversation with it. For example, if you have consistently disliked your stomach for years and find it hard to say anything loving about your belly (let alone look at it), this is where transformation begins.

Love your belly meditation

Sit quietly with your hands lightly touching your belly. Close your eyes and focus on your breathing, without trying to change your breath in any way. Just become more aware of the air entering through your nose and exhaling through your nose. Bring your awareness to your belly and turn your attention inwards. See if you can feel your belly from the inside out. See if you can bring your breath all the way down into your lower belly, feeling the belly softly expand as you inhale and deflate as you exhale. Begin to open up a conversation with your belly by finding ways in which you can thank that area for all of the things that it has done for you. Thank it for carrying your deep emotions, for being the softest pillow for your child to snuggle into as they curl up on your lap. Thank your belly for being the centre of your body's universe – the place where all wisdom, food, feelings and intuitions are digested. Thank your stomach/core for supporting your body and being a home for your reproductive organs. Thank your belly for giving you the opportunity to belly dance (even if you don't). Thank your gut for housing seventy to eighty percent of your immune system. Our bellies are extraordinary. They were never meant to be criticised, judged or tried to be flattened out like a pancake. Instead they were always meant to be loved, praised, listened to, felt, kissed, and held in reverence as the core of our being. When you begin to connect with your body in this kind, appreciative and loving way, you begin to rekindle a divine relationship between your mind, body, heart and soul. Your words and touch begin a healing that is so profound that it changes the way you feel about your body and your life forever. When you have looked at yourself with love, when you acknowledge your body with gratitude, you create a dynamic partnership which forms the basis for every other relationship in your life. We so often give our hearts to other people in our lives and forget to give them to ourself.

Belly Talk – A Body Love Meditation for you to practice

Allow yourself to feel a deep and genuine gratitude for your belly. As you connect more consciously with your belly, let it know that you are here.

An example dialogue goes like this:
Dearest belly, I'm here for you,
I'm so sorry that I've neglected you.
I'm so sorry that you've been hurt.
I'm here now and I'm not going anywhere.
You don't have to change.
You can be exactly as you are.
Thank you for being here for me, for loving me and supporting me.
I'm so grateful for all that you do.
Thank you for never giving up on me.
I'm listening.
I'm here.

You're safe.
I've got you.
I love you.

Love is found in the strangest of places

These were words that I found written in one of my diaries:

"My body, for so long I have struggled to get you right, hone you in and tie you down. You were only acceptable if you resembled some kind of photoshopped image I had of you in my mind. I ignored so many opportunities in my life because I couldn't bear to take you along as my "plus one!" I was ashamed of you – to be seen in public with you. If we had to go out together I covered you in black drapes where your outline couldn't be determined and therefore no one could see the real shape of you – the burden I carried. I thought that people would feel sorry for me if they saw you. It was enough for me to feel the rubbing of my thighs and the rolls of my stomach. I reasoned that if I could hide you, then maybe I could pretend that I didn't have you."

But love is found in the strangest of places and as much as I tried to run from my body I always had to return. As much as I always tried to control, punish, cajole, bargain, discipline or ignore my body I always had to face it. Somewhere between my many varying shapes, sizes and disguises I began to see my body as a friend – an ally. I began to realise that no matter what I did to my body or how much I tried to ignore it, my body was always there for me no matter what. I noticed that no matter how much food I'd eaten on one of my binges that my body would fight to get me well again. I watched how my body took the abuse I gave it and still got me up in the morning. There was something truly marvellous and humbling about the way my body never deserted me. I began to feel a sense of gratitude. I began to wear my body a little better. I stood up a little taller and breathed a little deeper. I moved my body out of the black shrouds and began to flirt with a pink, "off the shoulder" number. I began to look at my body as if it were someone I cared about. I thanked it quietly for standing (literally) by me through everything I had put it through. Through all of the name-calling, the demanding it should be something it could never be. I felt a stirring of compassion and gratitude. I began to look differently at all of the other bodies that I had always wished were mine instead of the one I had and wished them well. I began to see through the tricks and fakery, the lighting, the brighteners and whiteners of the airbrushed images I had once coveted. I began to look for the soul inside these fabulous but one-dimensional works of glossy art. Gradually, I began to befriend my body by being able to be grateful for all it gave me and the love it never failed to show me. And slowly and rather magically a gentle peace began to exist between us, body and soul, soul and body. My body and I were, at last, an item!

All that really matters...

A note from your body
My sweetest you
One day you may look back as you are slipping away from your earthbound time here and realise how magnificent I was.
Will you look back and wish with all your heart that you could have the young me back, even though I didn't seem good enough at the time?
Will your heart ache for all those opportunities that you didn't take because you compared yourself to others and felt not "good enough?"
Or, will you simply thank me for a fabulous life, well lived in ME, your most amazing, loving and awesome body?
(Hint – the latter sounds good to me!)

From your marvellous body! x

At the end of our days will it be the car we reach out for or the house? Will it be the accolades for the work we've done or how much money we have in the bank? Is it our status that we will want the most? Will we still be seeking someone else's approval? In a recent survey the number one top regret of the dying was that they wished they had lived a life that was true to them and not the life others expected they should live. What was really sad was that many did not realise until the end that happiness and love is a choice. They had stayed stuck in old patterns and habits. The so-called "comfort" of familiarity overflowed into their emotions, as well as their physical lives. Fear of change had them pretending to others, and to their selves, that they were content, when deep within, they longed to laugh properly and have silliness in their life again.

At the end of our days all that really matters is love and gratitude. That you have loved your body, your life and the people in it. When the final minutes and seconds of your days gather around you ready to be breathed one last breath, all that has ever mattered are the relationships you've had; the relationships with others, the world, your life and your body! All that is important is the love you've given and received. All that is heard is the long satisfied sigh of your soul as it says, "Thank you dear body for holding me safe, the experience and the love. It's been a real pleasure...I love you. Until the next time...."

And when we prepare to leave our bodies and the home that has kept us so safe all of those years my *own* personal desire is that I want my last words to be Thank you. Thank you to my body, my loved ones, my life and this beautiful planet that I was so very blessed to walk on all these years.

The body beloved

It is always the body that is missed so dearly when a loved one dies. We miss their physical presence. We long to be able to touch their hands again or to be lifted up in the flash of their smile. We ache to look into their eyes again or put our arms around their shoulders and hug them tightly. It doesn't matter what their body looks like or how much illness may have eroded their flesh, we simply long to be in the company of this beautiful soul which is illuminated by their beloved body. We cannot touch the soul, but we can touch our loved one's face or hold their hands. I remember tracing the lines on my mothers hands after she had suffered a massive stroke. Never before was I so aware of how her hands looked and felt. As I touched the paper dry skin and noticed the blueness of her veins as they snaked through her translucent skin, I tried to memorise this moment. I knew that we didn't have long together and I wanted every single feeling and memory of her to be etched in my mind and my being forever. When we are faced with moments of our own mortality most of us will choose the body! It is in those moments of facing a serious disease or suffering an accident that may be life limiting that we will do anything to stay another moment in our precious body. No matter how much we may have blamed or judged our body in the past for not being the body we wanted or the "perfect" body. At these times we suddenly realise that we don't want to be without our body – no matter what! As in many things in life, we often don't fully appreciate it until its very existence is under threat. I had taken for granted the fact that I could dance for years. It was only when I couldn't walk that I found a newfound appreciation for my legs. It no longer mattered that I couldn't get into size 10 jeans, all I really wanted was to be able to get out of bed and into my life again!

Say "THANK YOU!"

As you begin to move into your day, say a little "thank you" for another day of your wonderful life to be experienced in your incredible body. We are so privileged to be alive. It is such an incredible gift. In my own life I am aware of so many people who would give anything for another day to be able to enjoy a cup of tea, go to the shops, walk out in nature or just be able to hug the people they love. They don't have this luxury called life. I would give anything to be able to spend another Sunday afternoon with my mum just laughing and chatting over endless cups of tea. Such a simple sweet pleasure that I missed so much when she was no longer here. So lets embrace the moments of our life and make it our mission to live fully and deeply whilst we ARE ALIVE!

Begin to create more of an awareness of all of the everyday things your body allows you to experience. Begin to cultivate the attitude of gratitude by practicing saying "thank you" to all the hundreds of things that your body gives you. So often we simply take our body for granted. We ignore the simplest and smallest of actions and experiences we have through our bodies. Thanking your body begins to allow an inner shift to take place and a gentle healing to begin. It deepens the relationship you have with your body by acknowledging all that your sweet body does for you and gives you.

Here are some fabulous reasons for thanking your body!

Thank your body for being your home – your soul's address.
Thank your arms for embracing, opening, lifting and hugging.
Thank your hands for touching, creating and holding all you love.
Thank your skin for feeling, glowing and protecting you.
Thank your eyes for seeing and beholding the beauty in this world.
Thank your ears for hearing and listening to the soundtrack of your life.

Thank your lips for kissing and forming shapes for the words you speak.
Thank your mouth for eating, smiling, and speaking your truth.
Thank your tongue for tasting and savouring the edible moments of your life.
Thank your spine for supporting, twisting, bending and being flexible yet unbelievably strong.
Thank your belly for laughing, loving and creating a home for new life, new ideas and renewed health and vitality.
Thank your hips for dancing, wiggling, playing and curving sensuously.
Thank your knees for moving, bending, supporting and carrying you forward.
Thank your legs for striding, sashaying, climbing, high kicking, dancing and curling up on winter afternoons in front of the fire.
Thank your shoulders for balancing, rotating, rolling and being the most mobile joint in your body.
Thank your feet for connecting, arching, jumping for joy, pointing, flexing, supporting your body's weight and lovingly cushioning every step you take – for grounding you and being such strong foundations.
Thank your eyelashes for fluttering and protecting your beautiful eyes.
Thank your cells for growing, building more of you, transmitting information and being able to "listen" to what you say and create what you desire!
Thank your heart for beating around 115,200 times a day (over 3 billion heartbeats in a lifetime!) Thank it for guiding you, whispering it's loving wisdom and knowledge to you.
Thank your lungs for breathing in all of your beautiful life
Thank your blood for lovingly flowing throughout your body. For fighting infection, keeping you warm, circulating the nutrients of food, love, thoughts and beliefs into every part of your being

Thank you is such an easy and delightful word to slip into conversation with your body. Say thank you after every workout you do, every meal you eat, every moment of joy you experience. Say thank you to the different parts of your body and acknowledge them for what they do. Deepen the connection with your body by thanking it at every opportunity you have.

End your day with a Thank you note!

Just as you began the day with your morning intention, it is a beautiful practice to end your day with a note of gratitude to your body. Buy yourself a note book or journal and dedicate it to appreciating and being grateful to your body. I love to take an ordinary diary and decorate the front cover with pictures that inspire and reflect what I love most in my life. I cover the front of my diary with pictures of roses tumbling from old stone brick garden walls, dripping sunsets of summer, white sandy beaches kissing the shores of a turquoise sea. I cut out pictures from magazines, books or postcards that I find. I decorate the inside pages with photos of the people I love, my beloved animals, my home, quotes that I find inspiring and I even stick in pieces of ribbon or wrapping paper from Christmas or birthday gifts. It gives me huge pleasure to turn an ordinary diary into a personal work of art. Every time I open it I am reminded of the beauty and magnificence of life and it calls me to give thanks to my body for enabling me to be here to appreciate it. Just doing this shows you care. It's about taking time to honour everything in your life as an expression of your love and appreciation of you.

Writing down your words of thanks has been shown to have significant effects on your entire well being. Recent studies showed that people who kept a gratitude journal caused participants to report the following positive health and wellbeing effects:

> "16% fewer physical symptoms, 19% more time spent exercising, 10% less physical pain, 8% more sleep and 25% increased sleep

quality". *(Emmons, R. A., & McCullough, M. E. (2003). Counting blessings versus burdens: An experimental investigation of gratitude and subjective well being in daily life. Journal of Personality and Social Psychology).*

The emotions of appreciation and gratitude are shown to induce the relaxation response. One study showed that patients with hypertension who were instructed to count their blessings once a week showed a significant decrease in their systolic blood pressure. It seems that gratitude is not merely related to well-being but it actually CAUSES well-being!

Linger longer in gratitude

Isn't it interesting how so often we keep repeating and replaying what went wrong in our lives or what isn't right about us? We go over a painful conversation or a difficult event. We talk about how someone was mean to us. We may even carry a grudge for years! And in doing this we bind those feelings and events to us even more tightly. We keep them alive with every re-telling of what happened. It's not the problem that's the issue, it's that we keep thinking or talking about the problem that causes more of the problem. We seldom do this with the things that have gone right for us or that we find pleasurable or beautiful. How often do you speak about the beautiful sunrise or the delicious cup of tea you had this morning? How often do you write letters or send emails of gratitude? How often do you look in the mirror and wish yourself a happy day and tell yourself what you love most about you? It's so easy to moan about the rainy day but how often do you linger by the blossoming rose in the garden just drinking in it's beautiful aroma? Life unfolds in the moment so extend these moments of bliss by spending just an extra ten seconds of time with them. And then replay the feeling and talk about it and remember the joy you felt. Love a little longer – stay with the feel good feelings, accept a genuine compliment and bathe in it a little while. Have what is good instead of wallowing in what has hurt. Remember, that whatever you appreciate, appreciates!

Gratitude tastes wonderful.

Just as with a delicious meal, make it your intention to savour gratitude daily. When you appreciate something, stop, breathe in fully and really let it sink in. Notice any emotions you are feeling. Tune into how your body responds when you are feeling that deep sense of appreciation. You might detect a sense of freedom and openness in your chest; you might feel lighter and more relaxed. Use all of your senses to capture the moment. Your life is not a rehearsal: don't let this moment just slip by unnoticed. When you think about your body or look at yourself in the mirror, be grateful! This is where you live! Without your beautiful body you wouldn't be here.

I was deeply moved by one of my clients who had witnessed the devastating Tsunami in Thailand several years ago whilst she was on holiday. She recounted her feelings with such emotion: "*It just put everything into perspective for me. I've spent my whole life feeling unconfident and full of hatred for my body, yet when I saw those poor people trying to escape for their lives, I thanked the Lord that I was still here. My own body issues simply paled into insignificance as I realised that I was one of the lucky ones – I still had my life! It seemed somehow sacrilegious to moan about my heavy legs or bad skin when there were people who would have given anything to have lived another day – regardless!*"

The people whose lives were taken as a result of that day didn't get another chance to enjoy their lives. Many spent their final seconds desperately trying to get messages to their loved ones to tell them they loved them one last time. In the last moments of our lives it is not the size of our hips or the shape of our bodies that we are concerned with. Our last moments are about love, peace and being able to let go with love and gratitude.

The Taming Temptation Technique!

Promise yourself that from this day forward you will take nothing for granted. Promise that you will awake in the morning and whisper "Thank you" for the start of a new day and new opportunities to embody the best YOU! Promise your body to treat it kindly – with compassion and unconditional love.

Whenever you are tempted to judge or criticise your body, stop and use the taming temptation technique! This is an easy and highly effective coaching tip that has helped thousands of my clients to transform their relationship with their body. Before you judge your body in any way say to yourself, "I am tempted to... (*put in whatever you feel tempted to do*) and add in to that sentence, however, I'm going to thank and appreciate it instead". So, your sentence might look something like this, "I'm tempted to dislike my body for not looking as I want it to, however, I'm going to thank and appreciate it instead."

Then find at least three things that you can thank and appreciate it for. This simple, easy and powerful technique helps you to become more aware of what you are about to say, acknowledge this and then offers you the opportunity to change your mind. It creates a small space between thinking a habitual unkind thought and switching to a more appreciative and grateful one instead. Essentially it opens up a new moment where you can choose to be grateful instead of grumpy, hateful or judgemental! This technique also works wonderfully well in every other relationship you have. The next time you are tempted to find fault in a loved one, stop and use this technique. The beautiful part is when you are able to find at least three things about that person that you love or are deeply grateful for. We cannot be grateful and critical at the same time. Compulsion and conscious compassion simply cannot co exist! When you are in gratitude you are in peace. When you are more peaceful you become more present. When you are present you are conscious and when you are conscious you are the CHOOSER of your destiny and aligned to the whispers of your soul!

5

ROMANCE YOUR BODY WITH FOOD!

To my soulful you,
Feed the part of you that hungers to be born, feed the whispers and heartfelt stirrings of your soul.
Eat your desires, your passions, your loves and your dreams.
Eat food that takes you to the banquet of your destiny and fill yourself up with life.
Consume with love, taste every bite, chew it over, stay awhile and savour the moments.
And when you are satisfied..when you feel the vibrational hum of foods that make you go "yum" walk away.
Give thanks and know there is always more...more love, fun, possibilities, opportunities, moments and experiences to nourish all of who you truly are.
Your nourished and fulfilled body! x

I have a deep and insatiable hunger. I used to believe that it was for food. Now I know that it was for life! A hunger that compelled me to eat to fill the voracious void in my soul. A hunger that hurt and took me to the edge of my own mortality. Live or die. Choose or ignore. Feel or numb out. Listen or lose.

My hunger has always been there. I managed at times in the past to tame this wild and gnawing beast within. I've offered it substitutes for what it truly wanted. Take this biscuit – it's low in fat and has no sugar. So have that and be satisfied. It will give you what you want and you won't put on weight. You could have five of these biscuits compared to the one you really want. Platitudes, placating and trying to please a soul that is starving for a life less lived doesn't ever work! It can never work! My soul was hungry. It had been hungry for years. But I could never hear the voice of my soul – the sad soft whimpering sound it made when I fed it substitutes. Your life cannot be substituted. It's not acceptable for the soul to be given a mediocre, tasteless, bland and safe life in exchange for the one that it truly desires. I had been on an emotional and spiritual starvation diet for most of my life. The courage to be authentic is at the heart of every hunger. Will we give ourselves what we truly hunger for every day? In every bite of food and life we take we are asked the question, "Does this fulfil you and bring you joy?" Every day brings us endless choices of what we will choose to feed ourselves. Will we delight in the beauty of the morning and stop awhile to listen to the birdsong? Or, will we get caught up in the busyness of the day and forget to notice our own inner urgency to love and look after ourselves? Will we feel our feelings and meet the moment just as it is without our old "stories," fears and judgements? Or will we drown it all out with yet another hunk of cheese or try to placate our passion with another piece of pie?

Eating the Soul Awake!

When did we become so disconnected from what it is we truly desire and who we authentically are? When did nourishing ourselves become something of a guilty pleasure rather than an absolute necessity and joy? The roots and answers to this lie deeply embedded in our culture, upbringing, thought systems, politics, beliefs and families of origin. Obesity rates are soaring and children as young as twelve are being diagnosed with type 2 diabetes. Eating disorders are on the increase in both men and women and cosmetic surgery rates continue to climb as more and more people search for ways that they can fall in love with themselves. Isn't it extraordinary that when you walk into the supermarket there are thousands of "food like" products that call to us from the shelves but most of it is not *real* food. Even if you have never suffered from an eating disorder much of our relationship with food is disordered and laced with guilt, confusion and misunderstanding. What to eat and what not to eat are daily topics of conversation and are written about endlessly in magazines and diet books. Every day there is a new food fact. Every month there is some type of new diet proclaiming that this is the diet that ends all diets.

Our relationship with food has changed beyond all recognition. No longer a simple way to fuel, nourish, replenish and sustain our body, food has become a way of distracting from living our most authentic life. We eat to escape, medicate or distract ourselves from the sweet small sound of our souls whispers. We eat our feelings down and deny our talents and creative impulses. It's so much easier to pick up a pastry instead of a pen. Instead of following and honouring our creative urges we subdue them with "food like" fillers. There are hundreds of reasons why we eat. However the only real (or authentic) reason to eat is because we are physically hungry and require food to sustain us and refuel our energy. Food has become either a magic wand or a secret weapon. There are many reasons why we eat. We eat to stop the world from hurting, to stop the war, to stop ourselves from feeling the pain of so much chaos, death and destruction that we see on the news every day. We eat because we think we're not good enough, smart enough, talented enough, loved enough, attractive enough or creative enough. We eat to silence our voice or the voices of others. We eat to deny our passions and dreams.

We eat because it's breakfast and some magazine said that we should *always* eat breakfast! We eat to protect our selves from others or our self. We eat because we're bored, happy, confused, anxious, sad, lonely, angry, fearful or depressed. We eat because we might be hungry later. We eat because it's too cold, hot or somewhere in-between. We eat our dreams and desires down one heart stopping chunk at a time. We eat in secret, too ashamed for anyone else to see our inadequacies. We eat to hide our true hunger. We eat to keep others away. We feed ourselves the great excuses – who wants that spine tingling, all consuming passionate relationship anyway? "Love is so over rated" we tell ourselves as we pick up another bun! We eat to excuse ourselves from living. Food is our "get out" note. *Please excuse us from life today, we're just not feeling up for it!* We eat to rebel and show the world how angry we are, only we don't really want to offend anyone else or interrupt their busy schedules so we inflict pain on ourselves as bolt down three packets of crisps, a tub of ice cream and a jammy donut!

We eat because we're too afraid to stop eating – "who am I without the food? What greatness could I possibly become?" We eat to hide. We eat to become someone else's vision of what we're *supposed* to be. We eat to give meaning to our lives – *I eat therefore I am!* The daily drama and struggle with food at least gives us something to do.

We eat our guilt, shame, joy, beliefs, love and fear. We eat because it's a social occasion and that's what people do! We eat because it would be rude to offend the cook who's slaved for countless hours in the kitchen over a hot stove. We eat because it's raining outside. We eat because we're raining inside. We eat because we're afraid of what will happen if we don't eat. We eat to keep ourselves the same as our sister, friend, partner, children, family, and work colleagues. Will they still love us if we allow ourselves to break free from the pain that binds us and allow ourselves to shine? Will they still find us interesting if food no longer dominates the topic of conversation? Will they include us socially if we no longer join them for a late night takeaway simply because the truth is that we're not really that hungry? We eat to stop the worst from happening forgetting that it probably already has. We eat because living our wildest dreams is something that other, more talented and gifted people do but was never meant for us. We eat because we always have – it's what we know and what we've learned.

We eat because if we didn't we'd have to FEEL life and all that it brings. We eat to stuff ourselves into a body of fear where we pretend that we feel safe. We eat because the food is there. We eat because we don't want food to go to waste. We eat to say, "I'll show you!" We eat because it's dinnertime. We eat because we can and who cares anyway? But most of all we eat to deny the truth of our souls calling. "Who me?" we say. "No, surely not! Who am I to write that book, sing that song, go back to college, fall in love, be a voice in the community or a dancer in a worldwide show." We eat our souls into submission trying to fill them up with physical food, not understanding that our soul hungers for something that food can never ever give us. Our soul hungers for a life to be lived, fully, wholeheartedly and without reservation. The hunger of the soul is the hunger of passion, joy, love, bliss and radiant, courageous heartful and heartfelt living! When you struggle with food, you struggle with the true and authentic nourishment and fulfilment of your soul! You can never eat enough of what you're not truly hungry for. When your soul is whispering to you to laugh and dance and take some time out of your day to cherish just being here, and you stuff down a biscuit instead, you miss the moment. When you're caught up in anxious thoughts of the future or regretting something you did in the past, you miss the moment. Whenever you eat when you are not *physically* hungry you miss the moment to connect with the truth of who you truly are. You miss the subtle (or not so subtle) feelings that are just longing to be heard, felt, acknowledged and expressed through you. So many moments of our lives are missed as we ignore the simple sweet calling of our soul and consume substitutes for a life less lived!

Food – the greatest teacher!

The story of our relationship with food is an epic tale of what it means to truly nourish and support who we *authentically* are. Food has become our greatest and most profound teacher in our lives and if we can learn and grow from the messages and the lessons that food brings then maybe we can fall in love with ourselves a little more. Maybe we can discover what it is that we truly hunger for. Because if food isn't satisfying us or giving us joy then what is it we truly need? What is it we are really craving for?

Breaking free from emotional eating

Emotional eating is a language of its own, like hieroglyphics or braille. However, instead of trying to understand it, we're more likely to try to ignore it or try to shut it up. It's interesting as even talking in terms of breaking free from emotional eating is actually the wrong way of looking at it. Our relationship with food *is* emotional. It's not really about trying to rid ourselves or free ourselves from emotional eating but more to bring our emotions to the table with us. To understand what is going on, to listen and tune in to what we feel and make loving choices based on what we truly desire. To do this we have to become aware of what our use of food is trying to say. What is the wisdom behind the urgency to eat two bars of chocolate when we're not hungry for two bars of chocolate? Our relationship with food is expressing a true need. Like any relationship, we need to learn and understand what it is trying to tell us. Once we can do this, true and lasting happiness and self-confidence are possible. Once we "get it" and understand the needs, desires and cravings that food fulfils, our need to eat our emotions down will stop.

Take a moment right now. Consider these three questions:

- What are the benefits for my apparently crazy/disordered/mindless eating?
- If there were absolutely good reasons for my emotional eating, what would those reasons be?
- If my weight/bingeing/compulsive/disordered eating could talk, what would it say?

What are you really hungry for?

What is it that YOU are hungry for? How will you choose to romance your body with the food you eat and the life you live? What is it you crave? What does it mean to be truly nourished – mind, body, heart & soul? Whenever we eat for any other reason other than we are physically hungry we are feeding ourselves some kind of a lie or an untruth about what we desire in that moment. When you begin to recognise this and the different hungers that continually show up and demand to be fed and nourished in your life, something rather magical happens. You begin to connect to your body's wisdom and innate intelligence in a way that fulfils every hunger of your being. What kind of a relationship do you desire to have with food and therefore your life? What are your deepest cravings, desires and dreams? What does it mean to love and commit to who you authentically are?

Eating when you are not physically hungry is like trying to fall in love with a marble statue. You can keep saying how much you love the statue and spend hours looking at it, talking about it and being with it but ultimately it will never give you what you want. It can never hold you, comfort or love you in return. It can't heal your pain, uplift your spirits, run across the open fields or soothe your soul. It can't go on holiday with you, snuggle up on the sofa or take you dancing under the stars. It's the same with eating food that you are not truly hungry for – it gives nothing back. There is a mis-match between what you truly desire and what you allow yourself to have. The result is that it ultimately leaves you feeling empty, frustrated and disappointed. It's not the real thing – it's a substitute. You can try to convince yourself that you can settle for a triple fudge sundae, copious packets of crisps and a tub of ice cream, but your soul knows better and will never be satisfied with substitutes. As we seek to fill the voids we feel within or stuff our feelings down to meet someone else's expectation of how we *should* be, our souls begin to starve. So many enormous, fabulous, magnificent, vast, unlimited souls are just waiting for a chance to run wild and free! The hunger of the soul is free in spirit and wild at heart. It gathers us up in its ancient knowledge and invites us to dance at the edge of the world. Safe in your beautiful body it asks you to truly feel the energy of the moment in an unbounded state of mind. This is the hunger of time itself. The yearning and craving of a soul's fullest expression longing to be expressed in your physical form.

The love epidemic!

There is much talk about obesity being an epidemic. However, perhaps the real epidemic of our times is the desire to be loved, to feel fulfilled, nourished, safe, loved and truly satisfied in our lives. When an individual or a population begins to eat when they are not physically hungry, there is something else that is hungering to be fed. There is something that is not being nurtured, loved or cherished. There may be some part of the person that has been "put aside" or "forgotten" about because it was not safe to be seen or expressed.

I recently watched a documentary on TV telling the story of a young man who had allowed his weight to climb to around 54 stone. As he lay in his bed, confined to home for many years, he spoke about how he would love to lose weight, get fit and play sports again. Beside him was a photo of him in his youth on the soccer pitch. He was beautiful, fit, strong, healthy and alive with the joy of being alive. This was before he had fallen in with the wrong gang and lost what mattered to him most – his integrity! As his relationship with himself disintegrated he fed his emotions. He ate to forget, to escape, to shut them up, to disappear. He ate to get away from himself and all that he was feeling. Ironically, at 54 stone and a prisoner in his own home he was now forced to be with the one person he had no time for. The one person he most wanted *not* to be. As he told his story to the interviewer, his fingers reached out constantly for the sweets in the open packet by his bedside. His large baby fat hands fed himself the sugary contents as he spoke. The interviewer made a comment that maybe he should start by cutting down on eating the sweets. His eyes glazed over like the glaze of the sweet he was about to eat as he shrugged his shoulders and popped it into his mouth.

What the interviewer failed to realise was that this young man wasn't feeding himself; he was feeding the resistance, the pain, the wasted years and the emptiness he felt inside. It didn't matter to him what he ate anymore – he wasn't there! His relationship with himself had broken down many years ago and even though he spoke of wanting to change he had lost the trust and belief that he *could*. And whilst this is an extreme example of how detached and disassociated we can become with ourselves I see this kind of disconnection every day in my coaching practice.

Obesity in my view is not the problem – it is the solution! My own weight protected and sheltered me through many years of my life. When I couldn't bear to feel the feelings that I had inside, when life felt too overwhelming, when I doubted my own relevance and light in this world, food was my "go to" saviour of choice. My weight provided the barrier and buffer that I needed. We are extraordinary human beings. We will always find a way to give ourselves what we desire – to do what makes us feel better. Even if what makes us feel better in the short term actually hurts us in the long term. Any kind of issue with food is simply a creative and genius solution to rectify the status quo; to make us feel good – to bring safety, comfort and reassurance to those areas within us where we need more love and cherishing. We are so brilliant that even our battles with food are actually an expression to give ourselves more love – if only for a brief nano second of time! The body is a chameleon, constantly changing its expression, shape, feeling and energy to match and align with the "story" that you are creating in your life. Whether you feel too big or too skinny, the only thing that truly matters is how your body *feels* and the sense of aliveness, vitality and health that you experience. Your physical and energetic shape is simply the out picturing of your beliefs, thoughts, actions and the relationship you have with yourself and the world. Your body is always responding to the relationship that you have with YOU! It's language is exquisite. It sends signals in the form of pain, joy, density, heaviness, lightness, tingles, shivers, excitement, anxiety and emotions. Every second of every day your body is giving you a moment by moment "printout" of how you are and if what you are doing, thinking and believing is working for you or not. What we need to understand is that you cannot judge a body by how it looks – only by how it *feels.* I have been thin and still hated my body and I have been a size 24 and loved every single inch of me and felt passionately alive, fit and well! It is the *relationship* that you have with your body which determines just how fabulous, loved, joyous and well you will feel! When you judge obesity as wrong, you miss the wisdom, message and the story of the body.

Food, Love, Politics and Weight

As governments search to find new ways to reduce the rates of obesity occurring in the western world, they seem to have missed the one simple truth that would radically reshape the world. Teach people how to love who they are! Show them ways that they can reconnect to the mighty power and truth of their unlimited being! Stop the shaming and bullying tactics of pointing the finger at those who "don't fit in" and instead offer them a way to reconnect with who they truly are! Instead of posters or Television adverts scaring people to death with fears of heart disease, diabetes, Cancer or some other obesity related disease, lets entice people to feel wonderful, positive and curious about *all* that they can be! My vision is to have programmes on television that show people HOW to feel empowered, rather than the endless TV shows that are based on bringing people *down* in order to build them up. Many of the "Bootcamp" type TV shows actually perpetuate the body culture of disconnection. The underlying premise is that you can only love your body or get rewards, success, acclaim and acceptance if you knuckle down, do what someone else tells you to do and treat your body as if it is a second class citizen. This isn't love, it's fear!

The message that comes across in these shows is that fat is bad, fat is unacceptable, fat is the enemy and the body must be whipped into shape at all costs. The participants are usually treated like children as they are scolded if they gain weight or fail to adhere to the demanding fitness programme. I remember watching one such show where the participants stood waiting to be weighed in front of the panel of health and fitness experts. There they stood, acquiescent and controlled with low self-esteem dripping from their downcast eyes. It made me squirm, as these brilliant, beautiful and brave beings were reduced to the role of naughty children standing before their very critical parents. Parents who should know better. Parents who demand that they do as they say and woe betide them if they don't. And if they should dare to speak out or assert their own feelings, thoughts or sense of identity, they are smacked down verbally with words that wound and slice as sharp as any instrument. One contestant dared to stand up for herself after being ridiculed for not reaching the seven pound weight loss target that was set for her that week. She defended her feelings, saying that she still thought that fat was beautiful and that she liked herself fat because she liked *herself.* Here was a lady with fabulous self-esteem and body pride. She wasn't going to put herself down for a few stone of fat. She wanted to lose weight for health reasons but it was clear that she wasn't going to deny who she was in doing so. At this point in the show the ripped, lean, fitness machine expert launched into her like a missile. He's programmed to attack and seldom does he miss. He called her a white whale and denounced her body as unattractive and ugly. How very encouraging. How very supportive and understanding of someone who is doing her best to make positive changes in her life!

So, they lose weight. They have no choice. Under the bullying regime the weight is lost. But so too is their self-esteem and positive body image. It's a trade off – you play the game or you get out. The sad truth is that these participants can't win because at the end of the day they have the one thing that can be used against them – their fat! The main problem with these type of shows is it fails anyone who has ever felt the pain and distress of being overweight and not fitting in. It fails because it dismisses the person behind the weight. It seeks to control and intimidate rather than inspire, educate and motivate! Once we begin to view our body and our relationship with ourself in a new, loving and healing way, we will change! The more we choose to love our self and our body, the more we will make choices based on that love. This is radical because when you truly love everything about you, YOU become the expert of YOUR life! You no longer put yourself down or swallow down whole what others may think. You seek out the options that love and support you, rather than feel as if you are backed into a corner of fear. You take your time deciding what is right for you and listen to what your body and heart have to say before making any decisions.

Whilst governments continue to view obesity as a battle to be fought instead of a connection to be made, people will continue to suffer and struggle with food, health and their life. For me, my greatest learning was when I realised that no one could give me the solution to loving and taking care of myself. They could tell me what to do but until I was ready to take responsibility for the relationship I had with me – nothing could (or would) ever work! Whilst I continued to listen to others tell me what I *should* do instead of turning to my precious body and asking it's advice, I would forever live outside of ME! When was the last time you consulted your body about how it would like to lose weight? When did you last ask if your body liked the diet that you were just about to impose on it? When did you choose the foods you ate based on the feelings you desire to feel? When was the last time you asked your mind to come up with a selection of helpful options rather than just jumping on the first thought that came into your head? Have you *ever* asked your body or your mind those questions?

What truly nourishes you?

The promise of loving your body with food means that you become passionate about what truly nourishes you – mind, body, heart and soul! It means getting incredibly curious about what you want and fiercely interested in what you believe. It's about knowing what is acceptable to you and what isn't. It's about living your life in line with your values and learning how to allow these to show up every day of your life!

It's the ultimate loving nurturing relationship. You would

never try to feed your loved one food that they didn't want to eat. You wouldn't force your partner to eat when they weren't physically hungry. At the very least, we would ask our partners if they were hungry and what they desired to eat. When we begin to do this with ourself, we move closer to the truth of our entire being.

Broken promises

Marianne was a fabulous lady that I worked with. At 19 stone she was despairing of ever being able to lose weight. She told me that this was as big as she had ever been. She had reached her all time top weight and she was giving up on herself. After three weeks into the coaching programme she broke down in tears and said that her weight was now 19 stone 5 pounds. She had gained five pounds! I asked her what was happening? She said she didn't know; that she had just been eating all the high sugary foods that she knew were "killing her." She admitted that she had even bought a box of chocolate truffles before the session and had eaten five of them!

Marianne didn't believe, trust or even listen to herself anymore. She admitted that whenever she said that she was going to change there were forty thousand inner voices saying "yeah, right – I don't believe you".

The biggest key to Marianne's success lay in her beginning to trust in her word and start to believe that she would do what she said she was going to do. She could follow any number of diet plans but they would all fail. This was because the issue wasn't with what she was eating, it was with the promises she was making and subsequently breaking. Over the years she had begun to break promises that she made with herself. At first these were small things that she allowed to slip by. However, these small things began to eat away at her foundations; the relationship that she had with herself. After many years of accepting her own dismissive behaviour she no longer believed in anything that she said she would do. It wasn't her weight that was the issue – it was her word to herself.

It's not about the weight!

Once she started rebuilding her integrity and took responsibility for what she said, her weight became a non issue. She began to lose weight in an easy, relaxed and joyful way. Indeed her weight loss became simply a very natural by product of keeping her word and her promises to herself.

Marianne's story is important. It highlights how we all at different times have not kept our word to ourselves. And whilst the odd time may not cause too much concern, when it happens continually we stop believing in ourselves which can cause feelings of incongruence. On some level we know that we are not honouring ourselves and this feeling leads to disharmony, discrepancy, disconnection and distress.

I gave Marianne a coaching challenge which was to absolutely refuse to give a commitment to anyone (including herself) if she was not going to do it and see it through. I asked her to do this for the next ten days. Her challenge was to simply honour her word or not give it in the first place. The task was to keep every promise she made no matter how small, no matter how big. So, when she said that she'd go for a walk after work, that she did exactly that! When she said that she would take a proper lunch break instead of just working through, that she would honour this too! I asked her to call me every day to tell me if she had done this. She agreed. She felt scared and resistant about doing this. There was so much doubt in her mind that she could achieve this, but she did it. Every day she called me to let me know how she had done. Even calling me was a huge step in keeping her promises and honouring her word. At the end of ten days she reported that she had lost five pounds in weight. I asked her if it had been hard to lose. She replied that she hadn't really thought about it very much. She had been far too busy in focussing on honouring her word to herself and others.

Keeping your promises is integral to building a new relationship with you, whereby your word matters and you believe and trust in what you say. Either do what you say or don't say what you will do!

Know what you are hungering for – understanding the five hungers

Hunger comes in all shapes, sizes, ages, feelings, colours, emotions, needs, desires, wants, expectations, connections, relationships, jobs, environments, speeds, states, creativity, people and fantasies. What are you really hungry for is one of the greatest and most interesting questions that you can ask yourself. Most people don't really know what they want or find it difficult to imagine what their most authentic and happiest life looks like. Many people have bought into someone else's dream of what the best life looks like without really evaluating if this is right for them or if indeed they desire this at all! However, in order to know and truly understand what you are hungry for at any moment in your life you have to know and understand the subtle key differences between all of your hungers.

I have formulated the idea of five key hungers in our life that are always vying to be nourished or fed at any given time. These five hungers are continually flowing through our body, mind, emotions, beliefs, thoughts and energy systems. They are constantly evolving, dying away, surging up, snuggling in, demanding our attention or quietly snoozing in the background depending on our inner and outer environments. These hungers are like a river. They continually flow in and around our thoughts, beliefs, actions, experiences and are always being influenced by both our inner and outer environment. To what degree we may feel or become aware of our hunger is the intensity and speed of the current of the river. At any moment any of our hungers may be triggered into action demanding to be soothed or comforted, honoured or let go of. If we are in a peaceful state of being, both inside ourselves and in our outer environment we may experience little or no hunger of any kind. When people are in a state of flow when they are doing something they love or engaged in an activity that fulfils them completely, they may be unaware of any kind of hunger. You often hear people saying that they were so totally involved in the moment that they didn't notice the time passing. They often forget to eat or drink as they are so engaged in the flow of the experience of the present moment.

Equally, our hungers are often highly influenced and triggered by the currents of events that happen outside of us that have the potential to activate highly hungered states of being inside of us. For example, you may begin the day in a great mood and yet a few hours later you find yourself heading for the biscuit tin and eating urgently and mindlessly. What has happened in those few short hours to change your state of being and awareness? The answer is usually some kind of external influence or input that has directly triggered an old emotional pathway or mindset. This can be anything. It can be your response to a dark, rainy and windy day, a passing remark by a stranger or a difficult encounter in a shop. It can be as simple as turning on the Television first thing in the morning and being met by some unspeakable sadness or tragic event that has happened in the world. It can also be the way that you greet your self every morning. If you look in the mirror and judge how you look this can bring up many hungers that all demand to be heard and fed. Every day of our life we are constantly being influenced and shaped by our inner and outer world in millions of different ways. These are the under currents of your life and this is what drives and activates the intensity, speed and flow of the river of your hungers. These hungers continually shape and inform us in the moment as to what we may need. Learning to navigate the flow of the river and the currents that flow through it are the keys to being able to take charge of how you will truly nourish ALL of you.

The Five Hungers!

Learning the differences between all of these five hungers is the key to being able to give yourself the authentic nourishment you need at any one time. The five hungers are as follows:

Physical hunger

Physical hunger often happens slowly over a period of time. It is often the easiest of the five hungers to spot, because it's messages are undeniable. However, for many people it can take some time and practice to really be able to tune into what their physical hunger truly feels like. This is because we are so rarely hungry these days. Many people simply don't know what it feels like to be hungry anymore because they never allow themselves to be. Physical hunger can be felt in many areas of the body including the belly, and the head. Many people will experience a loss in focus or concentration when they are physically hungry. Physical hunger can be experienced as a gnawing or a grumbling or rumbling in the belly and it grows with intensity until you eat something that truly satisfies you. Physical hunger twists and turns and changes every day depending on what you are doing and how much physical energy you are expending. It also changes with the amount of sleep or rest you are getting, your age, weight or medications you are taking. Physical hunger is simple and basic. It is the authentic hunger of the body of your being. It is the root hunger of the chakra system (subtle energy fields of the body) and it demands to feel connected, safe, grounded, secure, strong, reassured and that there will always be enough food to go round. Your physical hunger grounds and connects you to the earth in the most basic of ways. It invites you to eat to continue your life and continually reinvent and reshape your body. When you honour your body's real, authentic, physical hunger with food that inspires and truly nourishes hunger, you allow your body to feel safe, connected, heard, felt, grounded and deeply fulfilled. There are many levels of physical hunger that ebb and flow throughout your day. Physical hunger moves from desiring a small amount of food to requiring larger amounts at different times of the day. The key is to notice how your own hunger changes and informs you about what your body really needs and desires. It's important to recognise and honour the way your physical hunger flows and moves through you. For example some days you may feel that you desire to eat "heavier" foods because your body needs to feel more grounded or full. Other days, you may be content with foods that are light and juicy, which reflect your body's state of being. Even changing the climate you are in will dramatically alter your body's expression for food.

Physical hunger cannot be predetermined.

You cannot know in advance how hungry you will be or what your body will truly and intuitively desire to eat. And yet, this is exactly what many people do day after day as they eat according to the clock (it's 1.00pm. It's lunchtime, so I *should* eat). Many people begin their day with a hearty breakfast because they read somewhere that this is what they *should* do and yet they aren't even hungry at 7.00am in the morning. Every single day your physical hunger needs will change according to your emotional state of being, your energy output, your tiredness levels and your state of health. When we eat when we are not physically hungry we begin to lose connection with ourselves and what we truly desire. We have stopped listening to the gurgling or roaring of our physical needs – our true body hunger and forced ourself instead to comply with some script that has nothing to do with our own personal story of hunger or life. Just the idea of eating only when you are physically hungry can bring up a lot of fear in people. It did for me too! I had been so conditioned to ignore my own actual signals for food that the thought of trusting or even listening to my own body was extremely terrifying. How could I even dream of going "off plan?" The idea scared and also thrilled me. However, underneath the fear there was a whisper of excitement that felt free, liberated and in line with my own authentic truth.

I made a decision to allow myself to eat whatever I wanted. I began to shop intuitively. Every shopping experience brought me into contact with food in a different way than I had ever experienced before. When I gave myself permission to have anything I wanted, the question became, "What do you *really* want?" My fear was that I would disappear into a vat of ice cream and never be seen again, and yet this was so far from what actually happened. What I learned was that it was my *mind* that demanded the ice cream, not my body. Whilst my body might enjoy a bit of ice cream, it also craved other foods. I discovered that my body really wanted Beetroot! I hadn't eaten beetroot for years and yet I began to seek it out and include it in my meals. I also discovered that my body actually didn't want to eat very much. It was my mind that sought to continue the over filling of my body. This was very clear to me one day when I knew that I really wasn't physically hungry and yet simply carried on eating as I had always done. My eating patterns and habits were so ingrained and embedded that they simply wanted to play out the old story all of the time, even when I knew I wasn't physically hungry. It took a while to honour my physical hunger as the power of my subconscious mind compelled me to continue trancing out whenever I ate any food. It was as if an automatic switch was flicked on whenever I came into contact with food. I simply desired to keep eating once I had started. However, the process of change is much easier than we often believe it to be. The more that I became conscious of what I was truly hungry for, the more I could make choices and decisions based on my true desires. Every change we make is a process. I would go back and forth, managing and not managing, eating consciously and then slipping back into mindless eating again. However, this is all part of learning a new choreography. One step forward and two steps back is not a disaster – it's a cha cha cha! Whenever you find yourself doing this with anything that you are trying to change just recognise that you are in process – transition. You are learning new steps and that takes time and commitment. Trust the journey and what's more LOVE THE JOURNEY! This is what being ALIVE means! If you had it all perfect on day one, where's the adventure? Where's the growth, empathy, compassion, determination and understanding? Instead of loving yourself *less* or being critical when you slip back into the old patterns and habits, LOVE YOURSELF MORE! This is where you need YOU the most! Are you really going to abandon you now? Say to yourself, "It's okay, I'm doing so well. I'm so proud of me for wanting to be the best me!" Focus on what's great about you, your life and the changes you are making. How great that you had a slip up because it shows you the next step you need to take! Dress "failure" up as "feedback" and watch as your level of awareness, confidence, joy and skill grows! Change is exciting. Learning is empowering. Embrace both with a willingness to move beyond the predictable, safe, dull, mediocre and old ingrained habits. You know these so well. It's time for you to shine and leave a legacy of sparkles wherever you go.

Soul food

I had always intuited that my own relationship with food was far more than merely trying to lose weight or control my eating or appetite. Behind all of the issues and struggles that I had with food, I sensed there was a deeper calling. A calling that invited me to look deeper at what I truly desired in my life. Food was my own greatest teacher and has been instrumental in helping heal the disconnection I felt between my body, mind, heart and soul.

Food is one of the most powerful and potentially deeply satisfying relationships we can have in our lives. When you bring yourself to your food with genuine hunger, a relaxed and happy state of being and a desire to eat what truly nourishes you, you are fulfilled. It's as simple (but not necessarily as easy) as that! I say not necessarily easy because eating in this new way requires practice. Like any new skill, it takes a commitment to consistent learning and that is where the challenge is. However, the rewards in learning to eat authentically, intuitively and in alignment with what you truly desire is one of the greatest most fulfilling pleasures in life!

Mental hunger

The hunger of the mind is powerful, demanding, at times fearful and at others deeply peaceful, centered and relaxed. Mind hunger – especially the hunger of the subconscious mind can be extraordinarily powerful. It's a hunger that has been there since your birth (and possibly before) and all it desires is to be continually fed. One of the most challenging aspects of our subconscious hunger is that, for the most part it is invisible to us. We are so used to behaving, eating, experiencing and believing in the same ways that we learned when we were children that we have become blind and unaware of our behaviour or what may trigger us. Subconscious hunger can feel and mimic physical hunger. The greatest difference is that we don't experience the actual physical cues that go along with true physical hunger. We want to eat, but we're not hungry. We can be triggered instantly by anything. The smell of hot buttered toast, freshly baked apple pie, an advert on television, watching someone else eat, clothes that are too tight, tiredness, an argument, disappointment, the sight of cupcakes in the cake shop window etc. There is a mindlessness quality that goes with subconscious hunger. We're not present – there's no one home. Mindless eating is often experienced when you are busy doing something else. You may be at your computer and find yourself just reaching out for the biscuits or crisps by your side without even thinking about it. Watching the Television is often a common association and trigger for many people as they become lost in what they are watching and eat simply as a habit. The only way to break the associations and learned eating habits of the subconscious mind is to become conscious, aware and present. This is the realm of the conscious mind and the key is to re-learn a new way of eating, relating to food and what truly nourishes you. If mindless eating is harming and undermining your relationship with your body then mind-FULL eating is the most loving and nourishing answer.

Subconscious hunger – the hungering for the past

The extraordinary power of the subconscious mind is always demanding to feed it's programmes and conditioning from the past. It asks to be fed exactly the same meal in the same way over and over again. It never gets tired or bored because it's only job is to make sure that the automatic habits, beliefs, associations and conditioned mind set that you learned when you were a child get repeatedly fed. This applies to actual food as well as to all of the beliefs, opinions, mannerisms, thinking skills, and self-management strategies we take in. This is why it can be so hard to eat in a new, kinder and healthier way. As children we "downloaded" all the information we needed to know in order to fit into and become an accepted and loved part of the family that we were born into. We were fed our parents ideas and beliefs of what mattered, how to cope (or not cope), We learned what was acceptable in our family of origin and what wasn't. Every moment of every day right from the earliest stirrings of our tiny being we were drinking in and soaking up what it meant to be here and what it meant to be a member of our family. Food is the primary contact and attachment that we make as babies. It is instinctual and demanding. The new born baby will instinctively search for food and only be satisfied when it's needs are met. However, the real food for the subconscious mind is the food of habits and patterns. The subconscious mind records every feeling, behaviour, skill, belief, interaction and experience that we have from our birth to around the age of seven. It is learning how to "be" in the world. What makes this learning by osmosis style of education so powerful and deeply embedded is that up until around the age of seven years old, we have no filters or effective thinking skills to evaluate if what we are learning is true, helpful or even relevant. We simply swallow whole everything that is given to us. Most of us were fed a diet of positive and not so positive experiences. We were praised for certain behaviours and scolded for others. We learned what was appropriate and what wasn't and we began to adapt parts of ourself in order to survive and belong to our family. I remember being a naturally exuberant and wilful child. I loved to shout and dance and make a lot of noise. At a very young age we went to live with my grandparents. My father had died and we had nowhere to live and my mothers parents kindly took us in until my mother could find us a house of our own. We lived in a huge Victorian rambling house called Gorrick House. Much of the time I was scolded for being too noisy. I was constantly being told to be quiet and to stop running up and down the long hallway. I didn't understand why I had to be so quiet. What I didn't know at the time was that my grandmother was dying. She couldn't tolerate the sounds of noisy children or really any commotion at all. Everyone in the house had to tip toe around and spoke in hushed whispers for fear of upsetting her or causing her pain. I remember my mother sneaking me little treats to try and make it ok. I simply didn't understand what was going on but I was already learning that food makes it better and it wasn't acceptable to be exuberant or too excited. I was a big child physically and remember feeling that I was too much and too big in every other way too! Essentially I began to feed the parts of me that were deemed acceptable and starve my wild, free child of expressing her feelings and true nature.

The associations, memories, feelings, rules and experiences around food replay over and over within our subconscious minds. The key is to bring these subconscious (and sometimes unconscious) associations into the realm of the conscious mind. Once you become aware of a habit or a pattern around your eating, you have the ability to make a conscious and more mindful, authentic and loving choice about what you want to eat.

Body Confidence Coaching tip to help free you from the hunger of the past!

Whenever you find yourself hovering in front of the fridge or cupboard looking for something to eat and you are not physically hungry, try asking yourself this powerful question:

"Am I really hungry or do I just want to change the way I feel?" The important thing is not that you stop yourself from eating anything, but that you simply ask the question. The subconscious mind is a habit mind – a series of learned and felt patterns. It's a circle and a cycle of repeating behaviour and actions. When you ask this question you effectively pause that circle or cycle for a brief moment. Asking this question helps you to move more into the conscious present awareness of the moment. You may still continue to go ahead and eat but you have changed the habit or the pattern by asking the question. The more you stop and ask, "Am I really hungry or do I just want to change the way I feel" the more this becomes a new pattern. A moment whereby you give yourself the chance to decide if you *really* want that food or actu-

ally you are looking for something quite different and more nourishing instead. Questions are powerful. They help you to change your relationship with everything and everyone in your life.

The more *aware* you can become about what your intention is to eat when you are *not* physically hungry, the more you move into the conscious mind. The conscious mind is the creative mind. It has a hunger for creativity, new ideas, connection, understanding, authentic relationships, excitement and a soul-fuelled life! When you are conscious, you are present in the moment. When you are fully present, you can make choices based on your true desires and what really fulfils you. Conscious hunger is the closest to soul or spiritual hunger. It is the hunger of the moment – the appetite of NOW! It doesn't demand to be fed food, although it can help alert you to your physical sensations of being hungry in the moment. Being conscious is being awake and aware.

The hunger of the Conscious Mind

The food of the conscious mind is it's ability to direct your focus, using awareness and attention and also its ability to imagine that which is not real. One of the greatest ways that you can feed the hunger of the conscious mind is to use it to imagine all that you desire. See yourself falling more and more in love with YOU! Imagine how good it feels to live your life in a way that loves and honours your beautiful body. Whatever is thought about in the conscious imagination and intently focussed on, also brings up all the feelings and emotions that are associated with that image in your mind for you to experience. This is exciting because it means you are free to create whatever you want. Every single thing that we do begins first in our thoughts. Nothing can be created without some kind of a map or blueprint or idea of what that thing may look like. If you want to feed your conscious mind, then allow it to feast on a banquet of positive, wonderful, life affirming thoughts, images and desires. Binge on joyful ideas, consume vast quantities of uplifting thoughts and allow yourself to be feel truly nourished and overflowing with the positive, health giving life nutrients of courage, joy, peace, acceptance, gratitude, love and compassion. This is powerful when it comes to overcoming any kind of eating challenge or distress. The more you can imagine a peaceful, loving and respectful relationship with food, the more you are able to re-programme your mind from the conditioning of the past and self-hurting habits and behaviours.

Emotional hunger

Eating is an emotional experience. Life is an emotional journey. Your emotions are continually coursing and flowing through your body. Every thought you think produces an image. Every image produces a feeling that is in alignment with that thought. For example, if I asked you to think of someone you loved, you would bring an image of that person to your mind. The resulting feeling would be of warmth, appreciation, love, connection etc. If I asked you to think of something you feared, for instance spiders, the same thing would happen. Your mind produces an image of the spider which translates into a feeling of disgust or anxiety. The feeling then produces a corresponding micro - movement in your body. In the case of the above example, you may find your body contracting or wincing. Your heart rate may increase slightly and your stomach may feel tight or knotted.

Emotional hunger is a reactive hunger. It occurs in response to your feelings – any kind of feeling can trigger the urge to reach out for food. One of the key factors in emotional hunger is that it's not the feeling itself that triggers the urge to eat. It's the inability or refusal to be fully present *with* the feeling without stimulating it or shutting it down with food. Emotional hunger is urgent and demanding. It usually craves only certain types of food for example ice cream, chips, pizza, cheese, biscuits etc. The issue with emotional hunger is that it actually can't be fulfilled or satisfied with food. In physical hunger you are able to be more conscious of the cues that your body has had enough food. With emotional hunger you generally only stop eating when you have shut down or numbed out the feeling that you didn't want to feel. Or, you become physically saturated with food and simply can't eat anymore. Emotional hunger plays a huge role in how we relate to food. We can eat because we're happy or sad. We can eat because we are celebrating or commiserating. We can eat to keep ourselves going or eat to numb us out. There are as many reasons to eat emotionally as there are feelings. In people with eating challenges however, the price they pay for eating results in some toxic side-effects. This is often felt as feelings of guilt, shame and self punishment. This, then perpetuates the emotional eating cycle which in turn feeds in to the subconscious programmes of the past, reinforcing old messages, habits and beliefs.

Body Confidence Coaching tip - LOVE YOUR BINGE/EMOTIONAL EATING!

Whenever you find yourself having eaten food compulsively or emotionally treat yourself with the utmost kindness and compassion. Shower heaps of love and positive attention on yourself... love yourself MORE not less for having eaten when you didn't need to physically. You may not be feeding your physical hunger but you are attempting to feed another hunger in the best way that you know how! So, honour what you are doing! On a very deep level you are trying to find what would truly nourish you... look beyond the food into your behaviour and your needs....and allow the door of your consciousness to swing open.

Emotional eating first aid kit!

So often it is hard to stop eating when you are in the middle of a binge or emotionally charged eating. This is often the moment that we abandon or reject ourself completely. When this happens the best way to really show up for you and honour what you are doing is to decide that as you are eating the food you will enjoy every single mouthful! The tendency is to just bolt the food down without really even tasting it and to also beat ourselves up mentally. So do the exact opposite: Bring yourself back to *actually tasting* the food…if you are going to eat it anyway you might as well at least get some real satisfaction from it!

Say to yourself: I LOVE AND HONOUR THE CHOICE I HAVE JUST MADE!

Remind yourself that whenever you choose to eat emotionally you are trying to help yourself to feel better and wake up to what you truly desire and are hungry for! The fact that you *don't* feel better after a binge or eating what you really don't want is *actually* brilliant! Why? Because it's the greatest feedback (pardon the pun) that you can give yourself. It is telling you…*not this way! This doesn't fulfil you! Try again! Experiment! Explore! Change!* It continually asks you "What are you hungry for and what will truly nourish you?"

Loving and romancing your body with food means that you become aware of your relationship with food and how you use it. The more you love every aspect of how you eat or have eaten in the past, the more you deepen a loving, solid relationship with yourself. Realise that nothing about your eating is wrong. Nothing about YOU is wrong. You are exactly right in every single way. Every so called negative behaviour always has at it's heart some kind of positive intention. That intention is based on trying to help you feel better in someway. If you continually walked away from every upset or argument in any other kind of relationship – you wouldn't have a relationship for very long. However, when you turn around and stay to talk, to be kind and loving and open to what is really going on, your relationship completely changes. This is powerful! This is life enhancing and potentially life transforming! Forgive yourself for being yourself – it's all okay. You're wonderfully human. You are messy and magnificent and magic – all wrapped up in one awesome, extraordinary body and you get to have YOU for all of your life!

Social hunger

The desire to belong is one of the most basic of human desires. It is a desire and a hunger that seeks out journeys of connection, intimacy, relationship, appreciation, value, creativity and shared human experiences with another and with our world. And yet this eternal hunger for connection is also about feeling and sensing a need for something greater or bigger than ourselves. To belong is to be a part of something; a group, a family, club, community, social media group, another person, church, sports team etc. In ancient times one of the worst things that could happen was to be banished from your tribe. Left out alone in the wilderness meant that your very survival was at stake. Safe within our groups or tribes and communities we feel secure. However there is a great price that many people pay for the privilege to belong. Every family, tribe, culture or group has it's own set of "rules" values and belief structures. When we adhere to these all is well. However, the drive to fit in is sometimes so great that we lose our own individuality and sense of Self in the process. This is seen everywhere in life. Within religious sects, family groups, schools, work places and groups of all kinds. There is a currency of belonging. To be outside of the group can be a scary and threatening place. In trying to stay within our own social groupings, relationships and communities we may find that our behaviour and actions are orientated around fitting in because it feels frightening to stand out. This has a huge effect on the way that we use food. Food is a great socialiser. Many celebrations or ceremonies of all kinds revolve around people getting together to eat. But what if you're not *physically* hungry and are honouring your true hunger and refuse to eat that piece of birthday cake? Potentially just this small action leaves you out of the group. Eyebrows may raise as you decline the cake or comments may be made. Just this action of loving and honouring your body may make you feel extremely vulnerable to feeling loved by everyone else. It is here that we often find the greatest challenges when it comes to romancing our body with food. The dilemma is always around the question, "Do I ignore my body and feed it in order to belong?" or "Do I choose to belong to myself first and sit with the potentially difficult feelings of not doing what everyone else in the group is doing?" The answer to this question is a personal decision.

However in romancing my own body, I now choose to belong to me first! However this choice and way of being did not come without it's own issues.

I remember going home to visit my mum whenever I got some free time. It would be lovely to see her and we would settle down in the lounge to catch up and share some time together. She would bring out the cups of tea, biscuits and the meal that she had made specially for my visit. The first time I said "No thank you" to the meal was as if the cold north wind had blown in through the windows and turned a warm summer's day into a frozen winter. My mother's face fell. She looked utterly crest-fallen. She tried to persuade me. She told me that she had made it because she knew it was my favourite food. She told me how she had gone out specially to get all of the ingredients. I hugged her and thanked her and said that I wasn't hungry. She shrugged her shoulders and looked offended at my refusal. The wind blew strongly between us. I was aware of the patterns of the past playing out their habitual longings and throwing icy shadows between us. Food was a way that my family showed love. I explained that I was looking at ways to heal my own relationship with food and one of these ways was to only eat when I was physically hungry. She didn't hear me as she said, "But just a little bit wouldn't hurt would it?" In my mind I remember thinking that Yes, it would hurt! It would hurt *me,* because I would once again ignore my personal truth. However, all I could say was that I might be hungry later. She looked sad as she took the food away and put it back in the kitchen. I watched her little rounded shape shuffle back into the kitchen, her head was bowed, her shoulders rounded over and I felt this overwhelming guilt and love for this woman, my mother who had already suffered so much in her life. Part of me wanted to just rush up to her and grab the plate and eat it all down and tell her how wonderful it was and how much I loved her for making it for me. I felt so selfish, so inconsiderate. Surely it wouldn't harm me to just eat the food and make her feel better! The least I could do as a "good" daughter was to eat what she had spent so long in getting ready for me! The familiar "stories" flickered around in my head as I remembered the countless times I had eaten to try to take away her pain, to keep her company. For goodness sake, she had lost her husband – the very least I could do was eat what she had made me! I was reminded of how many times in my life I had eaten to please someone else. I ate to keep my boyfriend happy so that he wouldn't eat alone when he got in from work. I ate at weddings, funerals, christenings and other social gatherings because it was expected of me. It would have been *unthinkable* not to eat – how very rude of me! I consumed buckets of ice cream with my best friend after she split up from her fella. My eating showed solidarity and true friendship. Well, it did to her if not to me!

What was interesting for me was that I noticed that many times when I had eaten in order to "fit in" or do the expected thing at a social event, I would find myself bingeing later that evening. There was a sense that I had "forgotten" me and had not been true to me earlier in the day so it obviously didn't matter what I did or how I treated myself. The message seemed clear. I had broken my own promise to myself. I had put my own true needs last again in order to please someone else. I ate to keep the status quo going in all areas of my life. We do this with many other things, not just food but as we are talking about social hunger it is important to know and understand your own social hunger clues and cues. The question is, "Are you eating because you are physically hungry or are you eating to keep someone else happy?"

The underlying pressure of social hunger is often minimised or rarely spoken about when it comes to developing a more loving relationship with our body and our self. However, it is becoming more recognised as a real issue in our society. There is a Television programme which recently explored the food connection between couples and how they colluded with each other in their eating habits. As part of the show they were separated for ten weeks and helped to look at their own relationship with food. When they were re-united again, both people had lost weight and regained a sense of what attracted them to each other in the first place. Many of the couples featured in the series were experiencing difficulties in their marriage or partnership. In all the cases food seemed to be a major key. They were either using food to try to connect them together in a shared "pleasurable" experience or to try to numb out the fact that the relationship wasn't really working so well.

In terms of romancing your body, who you spend the most time with in your life can have a dramatic impact and influence on just how much you will fall in love with you! There is a concept that we become like the five people who we spend the most time with. This isn't to say that you don't have conscious choice in what you think, do or how you behave. You do. However, it recognises the fact that the people we have around us can be strong influencers in our own decision making. For me, this makes sense in terms of the energy that other people and myself generate and constantly move in. When that energy is, for the most part, positive, flowing and peaceful it is easier to be in a higher vibrational energetic state of wellness and inner peace. I think we have all experienced being in the company of people who are consistently negative, angry, depressed or critical. Their energy can be draining and exhausting to be around and often we may find ourselves "hooking" into their drama and beliefs. This is really evident in close family systems where the family members seem "locked" into each others lives, feelings and thoughts to such an extent that the edges between the individuals become blurred. This can often be clearly seen where someone gets angry on behalf of the other person (even if the other person isn't really bothered). The boundaries of the Self have become muddied and one person begins to take on the feelings of the other person. It can cause a lot of arguments and upset as we are not allowing or trusting that the other person is fully capable of managing their own feelings, decisions and emotional states of being. We have overstepped the mark, often with the best intentions in mind and within our hearts. We rise up in the name of love, wanting to "protect" the one we love, even if they have not asked us for our help. A good friend of mine told me once that she dreaded going home after work. She said that she was spending longer and longer at the office doing extra work because she knew what would await her the moment she walked into the house. I asked her what she meant. She told me that she would often walk into the house feeling really upbeat and happy about her day. She had been looking forward to going home and sharing her day with her partner and finding out about his. However, her natural enthusiasm would often be met with a sullen and disinterested look. Within minutes of arriving home, she would find her good mood evaporating as she spent time listening to how her partner had been through the "worst" day at work, how he was unhappy and that no one seemed to value him. She would find her own energy sliding down to meet his and usually the evening would end with them both ordering a pizza and downing two bottles of wine.

She realised that she couldn't go on living like this and yet she loved and cared about her partner dearly. She had suggested that he try some counselling or coaching sessions but he wasn't interested. She also realised that *her* behaviour might be adding into the problem and not making it better. She knew that she couldn't change him or make him feel valued, happy or loved if he wasn't willing to allow himself to. She also knew that she had to look after herself as she was becoming more and more miserable in the relationship. She recognised that his behaviour was now a pattern and the way that she responded kept the situation alive. We chatted together and came up with a simple strategy that might just help change what was happening. Every evening that she came home from work and found her partner in a down mood, she would lovingly spend a few minutes with him listening to what he had to say. She then said that she was going to go out for a quick walk and that they could talk about it later if he wanted to. She said how sorry she was that he hadn't had a good day, gave him a kiss and told him she loved him. She then put her trainers on and left the house. It was brilliant! Firstly, she had given herself some space to connect with her own buoyant energy and do something positive for her which honoured her good mood. Secondly she had honoured his feelings but hadn't disappeared into them! Thirdly, she had broken a pattern and a habit that was threatening the relationship and both of their happiness. She said that it had been hard to do as it was tough to leave him. However, she also realised that he could cope. He was a strong, capable man in his own right and she hadn't been giving him credit for this. She had thought that he wouldn't be able to manage without her but in reality, when she got home after her walk that first night he was just really looking forward to seeing her. He had been so surprised that she had gone out and not spent the next three hours talking to him on the sofa. It had shocked him. It had broken a pattern and for the first night in a very long time she didn't order pizza or have the wine. It's easy to go down into someone else's energy but the truth is that it is far more helpful and loving if we can invite them up into a more positively focused way of being. However, all of this means that you have to put your relationship with YOU first! You also have to be prepared to say "No" to what you are not hungry for and a big fat "YES!" to what truly nourishes and feeds you!

Body Confidence Coaching tips for recognising and managing social hunger

1. The main recipe for social hunger is "should!" Whenever you find yourself feeling that you *should* eat because it's a party, a celebration, a commiseration or because it's lunchtime and everyone else is eating, stop and tune into your own body cues. Ask yourself, "Are you physically hungry?" If you are then, join in and eat. If not, ask yourself "Are you eating to fit in to the occasion and is this what you truly desire?"
2. Don't let your environment dictate what you should eat! Remember that you don't have to eat just because others are eating. You are not letting them down if you don't eat. They are responsible for what goes into their mouth and body just as you are for yours!
3. You are not letting others down if they have prepared a meal for you and you are not physically hungry at that moment. Maybe you can take the food with you and eat it later.
4. Just because someone may offer you food, doesn't mean you have to take it. You are not rejecting them and this isn't about them rejecting you! Do not be

guilted into eating. This only produces more guilty eating and feeling guilty about the foods you eat!

5. Eating in a restaurant or café with others. Very often you may find yourself ordering food, even if you don't want to eat because you don't want to be a non contributing patron. You could just as easily order some mineral water or get something to go.
6. When eating out, if the restaurant/café doesn't have what you desire to eat, love yourself enough to go somewhere that does! Don't compromise your food choices. Don't settle for less when you are worth more.
7. Take time to prepare and think ahead. If you are going out then take the foods that you love to eat with you. Have a mini selection of foods that you love to eat when you are on the go.

F.E.D. = Feed Emotional Dreams!

Remember that romancing your body with food really means that you feed yourself love. You don't have to eat to fit in or make anyone else happy. It's okay to say "No!" and you can do this in a loving, calm and adult way.

Romancing your body with food means that you feed your own emotional dreams. Remember what you are truly hungry for. Ask yourself, "How do I want to feel?" Then ask yourself if what and how you are eating really nourishes you. Does it give you what you desire to feel? If not, you are moving out of alignment with your authentic self and potentially damaging your relationship with you and your precious body. The most vital thing in all of our lives is that we truly and utterly belong to ourself first. That we get to know and wonder at this magnificent human being that has been born in the shape of "us."

Soul Hunger

A note from your body
Dear Fabulous You
I don't really care about counting the calories...
But I absolutely LOVE counting the FABULOUS moments of living we share together!
Lets go for at least a million a day!
Hungry for love!
Body x

When you begin to look underneath the surface of your issues with your body, you discover the real shape of your world. You begin to tap into a hunger that is so deep and so immensely powerful and transformative that it takes your breath away. It is a hunger for something *more,* something magnificent and full of wonder. Something that is magical, bright, beautiful and fabulous that has us reeling in happiness, harmony and healing. It is a hunger that has resided in our bones for eons of years and is as ancient and eternal as time itself. Its call has been heard the world over and its message shows up every time we are about to eat something we don't want and are not physically hungry for. The question is always the same, "What will you feed me – what do you really want?" And the subtext is, "Will this truly love, nourish and fulfil you?" The soul has a unique hunger. It is a hunger that cries out for expression, love, kindness and true authentic nourishment. It is a hunger that cannot and will not be swayed by any substitutes because it is a hunger for the expression of the Self! It is a hunger for the person you know exists deep within you. If you have ever stood in front of the refrigerator late at night scouring the brightly lit depths of its heavenly interior looking for something that will satisfy you and yet nothing does – you know the feeling of the hungry soul. You also know that food can never satisfy the soul – it's simply not the right recipe and doesn't contain the right ingredients.

The hunger of the soul comes to us in callings, nudges, whispers, ideas, creativity, longings, aha moments, insights, moments that take your breath away and fleeting glimpses of pure "knowing!" The hunger of the soul is fed every time we catch a glimpse of who we truly are. Every time we notice the dazzling light behind our own eyes or in another's we are in the almighty presence of the soul. Every time we respond to our greatest longings rather than run from our greatest fears, we honour the call of the soul.

The shape of the Soul

We've all felt the surge of our soul when it's been allowed freedom to express all that it is. Even if it's only for a split second – it feels *so* good! It feels so right! We feel it in the sudden rush of excitement as we contemplate something new and exciting. We sense it when we are out in nature and feel a deep connection to something so much greater than ourself. We see it in a baby's smile and wonder what they are smiling so joyously at. We hear it in a song, we intuit it in works of art and great writing. The soul's call is creative and liberating. It speaks of a great truth and integrity – our truth and integrity. Will we follow the call of our soul which is so often expressed in the hunger of our heart? Or will we avoid it? Will we run from how fabulous and glorious our lives *could* be because we deem ourselves not worthy or good enough? The paradox is that although we hunger to feel that sense of being truly alive and awake in our life, we are also afraid of it. Afraid that if we truly listen to the soarings of our soul, the song in our hearts and the beats of our bodies that we may truly have to change. And in that change we have to give up something that we have built our lives and maybe our entire identity upon. I remember coaching a wonderful and dynamic man who came to see me many years ago. He told me that he was the CEO of a large and very successful business. He had the car and house of his dreams. He was blessed to have a wonderful and loving wife and two great children. He enjoyed three fabulous holidays a year and had a property in the south of France. Money was no problem and all in all he had done very well in his life. I was confused. I wondered what he had come to see me for. When I asked him he looked me straight in the eyes and said, "I'm unhappy – in fact I'm miserable! I have every thing a person could want and yet, I'm not happy. I haven't been happy for years!" He told me he wanted to know how to be happy. I asked him when was the last time that he felt truly happy. He thought for a while and said, "I know this is going to sound crazy because I've had happy moments...but the last time I felt completely and utterly happy was when I was sixteen and was in a band." He went on to explain how he had always loved music and nothing gave him more pleasure than to play his guitar and sing." I asked him what had happened to the band. He told me that they broke up because it wasn't realistic to dream they could make a success out of it. He said that his father had his career all mapped out anyway. He was going to follow in his fathers hugely successful corporate foot steps and go into the business world. As he spoke about his music his face lit up. He looked so young. There was a passion in his eyes and his voice was uplifted. I asked him how he felt and he said "happy." As we continued to work together, we explored ways that he could bring his love of music back into his life. Today, he has stepped back from the business, while still maintaining a supervisory role. He has set up a music school, giving children the chance to explore their dreams whilst honouring his original dream.

The call of hunger

Whenever we don't follow the shape and calling of our soul we may spend a lifetime feeling alienated from ourselves. The soul's hunger is a deep vast hunger that grows in intensity if it is not fed. It will only accept substitutes for a certain amount of time. And although we always have a choice whether we will follow our deepest longings, ideas, creativity and passions – the pain of not nourishing our innermost dreams may be too painful to bear. When I was three, I knew exactly what my soul wanted to do. I wanted to dance! That was it! And so I danced. I danced everywhere and anywhere that I could. I copied the dancers on television and studied books on dance. I went to classes and loved every moment of this soul full activity. Until, that is, I got told that I was too fat to dance. That my body needed to be thin to be a dancer. That I couldn't get into the dance school of my dreams if I didn't lose weight. Suddenly my focus was on my weight and how thin I needed to be before I would be allowed to feed my soul's passion. My path became muddy, I found it hard to focus. I entered the world of diets and calories, weighing and scolding. I judged myself on how much I had lost in weight and kept pushing myself to do more and eat less. My love of dance began to fade as my hatred of my body began to grow. I was out of kilter and out of sorts. I tried all of the diets and only really lost more of my true self with every one I tried.

I had lost my way and felt completely abandoned in a wilderness of broken promises, starving days and restless nights. My way back to me and my love of dance and movement was slow and steady. My soul had not given up on me. The whispers and calls were still there. I just had to learn how to listen to them and then have the courage to take little baby steps of action towards it. Our souls have a shape of their own – they have a life force and energy that longs to be fed. They have an immense joy that hungers to be felt and a glorious voice that aches to be heard. Every single soul has a gift that desires to be noticed, enjoyed and shared with the world.

The hunger of the soul is the hunger to be the fullest expression of who you are. The soul invites you to answer the following questions about who you are and what is the meaning of your life:

- What is it that excites you, whispers to you, calls to you and has been there all of your life?
- What are you willing to give up to ensure your own unfolding?
- Where do you hold back?
- Where do you leap forward?
- What is right for you?
- Where are you willing to be led?
- What must you absolutely have in your life and without it something within you withers?
- What is the story that you have not yet told, but must be told?
- At the end of your days, what is it that you would most regret if it was left undone?

The hunger of the soul speaks its cravings from many directions. It shows up in the form of synchronicities or "chance" meetings. You may hear or read something that ignites the flame of a hunger within you and your life is not the same. It may show up in those strong feelings of envy, or jealousy whereby you look at what someone else has achieved and you feel a pang of pain. Wherever we feel a tug in our hearts there is the calling of our soul. At the deepest level this hunger is inviting us to become our whole selves. It demands that we commit to our purpose, passion and pleasure and keep our promise to ourselves. It's so easy to doubt ourselves and hold back but all we hold back from is being *more of who we truly are.* It's only us! And yet this can be scary! It sometimes feels safer to hide in the shadows of our potential brilliance and happiness – that way, we can't be judged, criticised or hurt. And yet, we judge, criticise and hurt ourselves simply by doing this. I did this for years. I held back, waiting for my life to begin. Waiting for that elusive time when I was perfect and I felt ready to do what I knew I must. The words for this book have echoed around and around in my head for years as I refused the urge to write them down. My fearful mind crept in with its taunting call of, "But what if no one likes it or reads it?" And in the past I would have listened to this inner voice until it got to the point when I replied, "At least I will have done it! At least I will have said what I needed to say and honoured my heart. I will have no regrets. It's the writing of the words that matter and the message this book brings. And if no one likes it or reads it, well that's okay because my soul will be fulfilled. My soul will be nourished and satisfied!"

The hunger for life...

Life is always asking us to engage and dance with it in the moment that it is happening. And although we may so desperately want to dance with our lives we make excuses. We say, "not now, it's too late, I'm too old, fat, thin, in too much pain, too cynical, too set in my ways, too poor, too angry, too tired or just too bored!" We make rational excuses of why we can't have what we desire or be who we really are. We nod quietly to ourselves that all this "life business" is for someone else – someone who hasn't got the responsibilities or the life we've got. We make sensible reasonable excuses why we won't take life as our dancing partner and embark on the most passionate Tango ever experienced. We smile politely as life comes sashaying up to us, arms open, huge smile, eyes blazing, energy sizzling.

"Come on, take my hands," life says in its best most seductive way.

"It'll be fun – come on – I'll show you a few baby steps!"

"No thanks," we say, "I think I'll sit this one out!"

Sit this one out! This is our life that's calling and our response is so often that we are too busy, or not now or I'll look like an idiot if I get the steps wrong etc. And sadly we turn away and walk back along the path so endlessly traveled. Back to the safety of our sorrow, back to silencing the inner voice that is our soul that is crying out, "Let me LIVE! Let me FEEL without censure, LET ME WAKE UP and express the BEAUTY OF WHO I AM! As the spiritual teacher and author Wayne Dyer so eloquently said, "When you dance, your purpose is not to get to certain place on the floor, it is to enjoy every step along the way."

We silence our response to life - with every shake of the head, every cream bun that wasn't hungered for, every reasonable excuse, every "not now, I'm too busy," every plausible reason we could think of. How can you sit life out? It's impossible! As long as you are alive life will always ask you to dance. As long as you have a body, life will ache to be held in your arms and whisked around the dance floor of your dreams. As long as you have ears life will whisper to you to listen. As long as you have eyes life will entice you to see the beauty of "what is!" As long as you have breath, life will breathe flickers of fire within you. As long as you have a heart, life will always and forever touch you. Life asks you to LIVE fully, deeply, irrevocably, totally, passionately and wholeheartedly. Life asks you to be ALIVE for every moment that is YOUR life. This conversation is always being spoken – felt – communicated. The question is always: "Will you listen to what your life is offering? Will you put on the dancing shoes of your soul, whether they are tap shoes, ballet shoes, street kickers or just bare feet? It doesn't matter what you wear, the question is "Will you dance?"

Food relationship question

What do you think about and feel when you eat?

The reason that this question is important is because the thoughts you have mean that your body metabolises food differently. Simply put, if you eat with guilt, fear, stress, negative self-judgement or anger it makes the food harder to digest. Whenever you are eating make sure that you do so with as much love, pleasure, enjoyment and happiness.

Bite size dates with destiny!

Every time you eat is an opportunity to feed yourself more love, care, nourishment, joy and health. Every food choice invites you to make every meal a bite size date with your destiny. It asks if you will authentically show up in your life and truly nourish all of your hungers – mind, body, heart and soul. Will you eat authentically? Will you eat in alignment and awareness with who you truly are, what you desire in your life (your goals and dreams)? Will you eat what makes you feel happy, fulfilled and truly nourished? Will your food choices honour your personal values?

Bring your WHOLE self to the banquet of your life and show up at the table as the authentic YOU! Select the foods that make you feel alive, fabulous, beautiful, peaceful, energised and fully and totally nourished on every level of your being.

Every time you eat it's like a mini date with your dreams, desires and destiny. Every bite you eat brings you an incredible opportunity to meet yourself continually throughout the day. Every meal insists on experiencing the real deal and having an authentic relationship with food. It asks you to CHOOSE instead of following some pre-prescribed way of eating. Every single bite asks you, "Is this bite in your best interest?" Every taste you experience asks you if you can fully savour and delight in the moment. Every time you engage in the eating experience you are literally re-creating your version or story of yourself. When you eat mindlessly and unconsciously you repeat the subconscious story of who you were "taught" (or programmed) to be from your earliest moments on this earth. Whenever you eat substitutes for what you truly desire, you know you are accepting less and you know that this is unacceptable.

What's the story of your food?

Our relationship with food is integral with living our best lives and following our own unique path. Food is not simply just fuel but contains a story and an aliveness all of its own. Everything about our relationship with food is significant. It matters – how we eat, where we eat, what we think about the food we are eating, if we are eating when we are not physically hungry, whom we eat with, how much we eat, how our food was brought to us, if we are stressed when we eat, what we desire the food to give us etc. It's a two way street. We often only think of food as being something that we do to the food (i.e we consume it) but in every mouthful, our choices, feelings, beliefs, attitudes, stress levels and values will be reflected back in how the food becomes absorbed in our body and becomes more of us. For instance when you eat and you are not physically hungry there is some kind of a discrepancy, lie or disconnection that you are feeding yourself. The absolute only reason to eat is to nourish your physical hunger in ways that honour ALL of who you truly are, what you believe, your values etc. Eating when you aren't hungry simply flags up that some kind of disconnection is happening, a moment where you are out of alignment with what you are truly hungry for, what you truly desire and what will nourish you completely.

Was your food loved?

The story of your food is also key in this relationship. Do you know where your food has come from? How it was grown? If you eat meat, do you know how the animal you are eating was treated? What kind of a life did it have? Was it fed antibiotics, left to roam? Was it happy? At the end of its life, how was it slaughtered? I know that these kind of questions are usually things that people don't want to ask. However, more and more people are now waking up and asking these types of questions because they know how important they are. Everything in our entire life is about the relationship and connection (or disconnection) that we have with it, including ourselves. Food is what we put into our body. For me, it is vital that I know and am happy with what I am choosing to consume. It is key for me to be able to make choices that are based on not only loving myself but also loving and valuing the food I eat. It was for this reason that I have been a vegetarian (and now vegan) for over thirty years. It just didn't sit well with me that I used to say that I loved animals and yet I ate animals. Nothing in that added up as I felt I was going against who I authentically was. I desire to eat lovingly and be loved by the foods I eat. When you combine your own personal values into what you choose to eat, you begin to eat consciously and mindfully. This is true authentic eating. To begin this loving process you may wish to ask yourself the following questions about the food you are choosing:

1. Do I know where this food came from? (What country, area etc)
2. Do I know how this food was treated? What was its life like? What antibiotics, growth hormone etc was it given?
3. Do I know what exactly is IN this food?
4. Do I know if any chemicals or pesticides were sprayed on to the plants or vegetables I eat?
5. How were the people treated who helped produce this food?
6. How was the planet treated in producing this food?
7. Does this food make me feel good about myself?
8. Does this food align with my own personal values and dreams?
9. Does this food give me positive life nourishing energy, health and vitality?

When you eat consciously, authentically, intuitively and in a way that supports your highest ideals, dreams and wishes you create MORE of who you truly are. Your body knows what it wants. When you turn to your body for the answers it will always answer honestly and truthfully. The body cannot lie. It tells it like it is. However, the mind *can* lie and what sometimes feels as if it's the body that desires the family size bars of chocolate, the crisps or the tub of ice cream – it's really the mind. In particular the subconscious mind that simply wants to replay the old recordings and feelings from the past. Many people experience that feeling of being in a trance when they over eat or binge. I certainly did. It was as if something came over me and I disappeared into a fog of unconsciousness as I began to load more and more food into my body. My body never wanted the foods that I habitually binged on. However, my mind craved them because they were part of what it meant to BE me. It was what I had learned many years ago growing up in a household of grief and pain.

Looking back on my own very toxic and distressing relationship with food, I think I always intuited that there had to be some kind of a connection between who I am, what I feel, what I desire, what I value and care about and what I eat. I always had a feeling that my life wasn't always supposed to be about totting up how many calories I had eaten and how many I had burned off. I think I always knew in my soul that life was supposed to be glorious and the most amazing adventure you can have - full of laughter, love, health & happiness. However, whilst my focus was centered on losing weight and only eating foods that were "allowed" on my list I was stuck in a very limited, dense and fixed mindset. It was only when I began to make the connection that the food I ate directly mirrored my relationship and integrity with who I am as a person that I began to change not only my relationship with food but with the way that I lived!

I remember that I had an epiphany around my own relationship with food, which completely liberated the way that I understood the way I ate. I had been on a diet from the age of six years old. In my child's mind I found food confusing. Food was something I shouldn't have but also needed in order to stay alive. If I ate only certain "good" foods then I was "good" and I would lose weight. If I ate what was considered "bad" foods then equally I was "bad" and didn't deserve to be loved. There was great fear around food in my family as my father had died when he was only 35 from a massive heart attack. He was six foot tall and weighed around twenty-two stone.

His death shocked and traumatised the entire family, splitting us off into our separate worlds of loss, pain, sadness and grief. My mother who adored my father was suddenly left to bring up two small children with no visible means of support. She did her best and I always knew that I was loved. However there were many times when she simply wasn't there anymore. Physically she was present, however emotionally she had vacated the premises. Too lost and wrapped up in her own grief she turned to food to comfort herself. Food became something we all indulged in to soften the loss. I remember many weekends spent snuggled on the sofa with my mum watching the Saturday afternoon film, whilst we ate crisps and ice cream as we disappeared into someone else's life or fantasy. This was deeply embedded into every cell and fibre of my being and years later watching the TV would always be the trigger that would catapult me into full on binges. It was simply an automatic response. When the TV was on I desired to complete the association I had with watching television and eating. I was compelled psycho-biologically and emotionally to simply "run" and play out the programme of conditioned behaviour that I had learned as a child. The programmes of eating behaviour were already installed and during my life I simply reverted to the default system of eating that I had learned. As children we "download" everything we experience. We soak up the great wonderful joys of our childhood along with the not so wonderful times. We are like sponges for the emotions, beliefs and opinions of those around us and we consume these energy substances daily. Psychologists talk about children as being in the theta brain wave state, which is akin to hypnosis. They do not have the capacity to think in a rational or enquiring way and believe everything that is given to them with no judgement, question or filter. Children don't stop to ask if what is being said is really true. It is only later on in our lives (if we are lucky) that we "wake up" and begin to become curious about the things we have habitually thought about ourself and if we really believe this to be the truth about who we are. Generally this awakening only happens when our old habits, behaviour or self-limiting beliefs become too painful to bear a moment longer and we find ourselves in a crisis. These crises may be experienced through our relationships, health, finances or in addictive scenarios that we are unable to transcend and find ourselves repeating year after year.

Mixed messages

My mother and the rest of the family were concerned I would go the same way as my father if I didn't lose weight. Food was fearful for me. My mother would buy me "treats" and then comment that I shouldn't eat so much.

Whenever I was tired or cold my mum would say that I needed more sugar to "pep me up!" When I was older and came back home to visit I would be offered biscuits and cake. When I helped myself to a second serving of dinner there would be a clear disapproval and a comment to watch how much I was eating. If I lost weight there would be comments that I was getting too thin and I should eat some more. If I gained weight I sensed a great worry and disappointment and fear that I would die an early death! I realised that the message I had internalised around food was that I simply wasn't allowed to eat! Neither way worked. There was no peace or joy around food. Food wasn't safe and I couldn't win whichever way I looked at it! Loving my body and learning to romance my body with food by eating authentically and intuitively transformed my relationship with eating and how I lived my life. If food has been your "issue" then food and your relationship to it is also the way through – the spiral pathway that brings you back "home."

Romancing your body with food invites you to deepen your relationship with your body and become really curious about what your body truly desires. It asks you to become really conscious and awake around food, to identify your "triggers" to your old story and consciously and intentionally make a new choice. A choice that is based on your health, energy and dreams of whom you authentically are and desire to be. Every time you eat when you are not physically hungry you are in danger of falling asleep again into the old fairytale story of your childhood. To romance your body with food means that you consciously "grow" into the person you have always felt intuitively has always been there. Underneath all of the old stories, patterns, hurts and behaviours is the truth of who you really are. It lingers around the very edges of your being and whispers through the subtle arteries of your soul. It can never be lost – it is the core essence of you. It is forged in love and kindness and it seeks only to be acknowledged and fed by what you most desire in the deepest depths of your conscious being. You are not condemned to repeat the endless story and myth of your life and food is the most significantly nourishing way to bring you alive to the moment of NOW and the writing of your new story. This is exciting because this time YOU get to hold the pen and craft your own adventure. YOU are the one who decides what you will eat, where you will go, what you will choose to believe and how YOU will show up in this world.

When you romance your body with food, you are invited to make every meal, nibble and bite the most loving, sensual and pleasurable experience. Delight in the wonderment of feeding yourself what you truly desire and make sure that you include the following soul vitamins with each mouthful you eat. Whenever you eat you are consuming life with every bite. You are literally feeding yourself your new story one bite at a time. Nibble a sliver of sunshine, swallow a ray of hope, drink down the most glorious summers day, chew over a new belief, taste the newness of every moment, savour the texture of endless possibilities and allow your body to be energised, healed and loved by the joy and beauty you bring to every food experience.

Add these Soul vitamins to every meal

Vitamin A = Authenticity, Acceptance and Awareness
Vitamin B = Beauty (The appreciation of beauty)
Vitamin C = Compassion and choice
Vitamin D = Dharma (The purpose and meaning of your life)
Vitamin E = Energy and enjoyment
Vitamin F = Fun
Vitamin G = Gratitude
Vitamin I = Inspiration
Vitamin J = Joy
Vitamin L = Love
Vitamin P = Pleasure, peace and presence
Vitamin S = Slow and savour (eat slowly and savour the experience)
Vitamin T = Taste (Taste every mouthful fully)

Making a real connection with food

Every single relationship in our lives invites us to engage in a relationship that's real. A relationship whereby we can be ourselves and accept the other person for whom they are without feeling the need to diminish or dim our own light in any way. Our relationship with food can be one of the greatest and most transformational partnerships that any of us can ever experience. My own relationship with food has changed dramatically. Before making my food choices I will often fast forward to the outcome of that choice. The question that I ask myself is, "Does this food choice give me what I desire to feel emotionally, physically, mentally and spiritually?" The "old" me wouldn't have cared what I was eating. It didn't matter as long as I ate. I didn't have to *like* the food – I just needed to "use" it. I rarely thought of the outcome of what I was doing and even when I did, I didn't care. It is a wonderful feeling to take time to value yourself so much that you really DO care what you put into your body and if the food makes you feel how you want to feel. Ultimately it's about being able to hear the call of your authentic self and your true hunger. These days I desire to wake up feeling light and joyful and full of energy and vitality. I love the feeling of not being weighed down with food. I adore the way my mind feels clear and my purpose in life shines out. None of this is possible when I am making food choices that aren't based in love, care and respect for me. Essentially, the call of hunger is the sound of our own voice yearning to be heard. It is primal, ancient and full of longing. It is eternal and yet changes constantly in every moment. To hear *your* voice above all of the others – your family, friends, colleagues and society takes a willingness and a courage to completely trust, love and accept yourself and feed yourself what you are hungering for.

When you sit at the table, who is eating?

Each time you eat you are actively recreating your version of who you are. When you eat mindlessly or when you are not physically hungry you simply repeat the old "story" of your past. You are literally consuming more of the "old" you. You continue to eat your lies about who you truly are. Every time you sit down to the table to eat you have to know who is doing the eating. Is it the "old" you who is unwilling to move and go beyond the limitations of your past or will you bring your *real* self to the banquet of your life and make choices based on what you desire to feel and be. For those who have struggled with an eating disorder of any sort, the simple act of eating becomes a constant battleground. I remember saying that I wish that I didn't have to eat because then I wouldn't be met constantly with this struggle around food. Just the act of eating could trigger a binge or days of compulsive eating. However, my own freedom around food completely changed when I began to align what I ate with what I desired to feel, be and experience in my life. All of a sudden it wasn't about my weight or what I looked like that was the focus of my life. It was about how I wanted to show up in my life, the amount of energy and vitality I had and my personal connection and relationship with the food I ate. These days I still enjoy my chocolate bars but I now choose to eat sugar free, dairy free and gluten free bars. I have acquired a taste for dark raw chocolate and I love the fact that I can eat chocolate when I desire it with none of the old triggers showing up. Dairy and sugar were huge physiological triggers for me and just eating them would then trigger the old psychological triggers of guilt, feeling bad about myself and not feeling that I was really allowed to partake of this world. Interestingly, at those times I would eat three or four family size bars of chocolate in the space of a few minutes. I would never actually taste the chocolate – I just wanted the escapism and "comfort" that it would bring me. Today, I delight in really loving the chocolate I eat and allowing the taste to fill every part of my being with love and health. It's such a vast difference and so completely joyful!

Body Confidence Coaching tips on how to keep your promise of romancing your body with food.

- Make every moment with food special. Allow your

eyes to appreciate the food you are about to eat. Notice the smell, texture, colour and shape of the food.

- Take time to prepare or select the food you want to eat. Cook and prepare the food with love – the most powerful ingredient in the world.
- Eat slowly and savour every mouthful
- Notice the energy signature of the food. When you eat when you are physically hungry the food you eat usually tastes unbelievably wonderful. The taste of the food is heightened and every bite is simply delicious. However, you may notice that after a few mouthfuls the intensity and pleasure of the eating experience stops and the food begins to taste more bland or loses its initial impact. This is key! It is a signal to you that your body has acquired what it needs from the food. Many of us go on eating long past the point of physical satiation and satisfaction. We have been taught to clean our plates, to eat what is in front of us because there are people who don't have enough food in the world or for many other reasons. When we habitually do this we have moved into the old patterns and habits of the mind and have lost touch with our own authentic hunger and true appetite. You can always come back for more food if you get hungry later on. Much of our unconscious eating habits stem from a feeling that there won't be enough for us – that if we don't finish every piece of food on our plate then we won't have the chance to have that again. So much of our uncomfortable relationship around food comes from those ingrained feelings of lack or eating because we don't want to feel guilty or that we seek to please someone else.
- Ask your body what it would like to eat. Begin to learn how to tune in to your own body wisdom and get a

sense of what your body desires. Maybe your body desires something chewy, soft, sweet or sour. Perhaps your body only wants a little taster of something and not a full meal. Begin to ask your body questions about what it wants. After all, you wouldn't go into a restaurant and just order straight away for the other person. You would ask them what they want and allow them time to decide. Do the same for your body. It may take a little practice to really begin to "hear" or understand your body's replies. Sometimes you may get a strong visual image for the food your body desires. Other times you may just intuitively "know". Often there is a feeling of lightness or a feeling that leads you to something your body wants to eat. Play with this. Experiment until you get a greater sense of communication with your body. One interesting way to tune into your body wisdom is to think of the food (or hold it in front of you) and then just stand with your feet about five inches apart. Ask your body if it wants to eat this food. Be open to how your body moves. If your body moves forward the answer is usually a positive one. If your body moves or leans away it may indicate the answer is no. Moving from side to side may indicate that there is not enough information for your body to decide or that your body has no strong opinion either way. The key with body testing is to get to know which directions mean what for your body. Sometimes moving from side to side may mean a "Yes" answer so it's important for you to decide what movements feel right for you.

- Give thanks for the food you are eating and to everything and everyone who has been a part of your food's journey.
- Eat what you most desire to feel. If you crave more

health and joy then choose foods that make your body feel healthy, alive and happy.

- Make eating a pleasurable occasion by creating the right environment. Eating in a relaxed, calm and joyful way is key to how your body will digest and metabolise food. If you can't leave the office then bring in flowers that you can place on your desk or a picture of a beautiful scene you can look at while eating. You might want to listen to beautiful music as you eat. You may want to bring in your most beautiful plate on which to eat the food. You may decide to buy yourself a gorgeous mug or cup to drink from. Perhaps a lovely napkin or a candle will add the right feelings as you spend this time nourishing you.
- Make yourself a pledge never to eat when you are feeling stressed. It's like going on a date or meeting people when you are in a bad mood – it doesn't work. You won't be good company and the experience is deeply unsatisfying. Only eat when you are calm, relaxed and in a consciously aware and peaceful state of being.
- Make it a pledge that you do not eat with other people who make you feel uncomfortable, judged, anxious or stressed. If you ever have to eat when the company around you is less than optimal, then talk to your body gently to create a loving inner environment and space. Say to your body, "Thank you for being here. Lets pull together to create our own delicious state of being. All is well." Eat lightly and allow your focus to be on your feelings. Breathe in peace and stay quiet and focused on the food and what you are creating by this loving exchange of energy. I remember meeting a friend of mine for lunch one day. We had arranged to meet at a little restaurant that we both knew and had been to

before. As she walked in she seemed slightly nervous and off kilter. I asked her what was wrong and she replied that she wasn't quite sure but that she didn't feel comfortable eating here. She asked if I minded going somewhere else. Although I was surprised I said I was fine with going elsewhere. We walked down the street and found another restaurant that, this time, she felt completely happy in. She was right – the energy in this restaurant was different from the one we had just been in. We had a lovely meal and both left feeling happy, fulfilled and buoyant.

- If you find that you eat foods that you weren't physically hungry for or that you indulge in your old patterns of being and ways of eating that don't support you – forgive yourself and move on! Remember that this is about developing a new relationship with your body. Beating yourself up mentally or feeling guilt or shame that you didn't manage to keep your promise only creates more disharmony and disconnection. The best relationships are built when we can learn from our old behaviours, love ourselves more and simply make it our intention to stay consciously aware next time. Your body will forgive you too – it's okay, all it really desires to know is that you are doing your best and that it is loved!
- Divine Dining – for those of you who would like a little more divine dining, you may want to invite your dining angel to join you! Invoking the power and guidance of your own food angel or "energy being" is a simple and magical way to transform every dining experience into a divine date! Ask your food angel to help you become more conscious with your body. Bless the food and make this a heavenly experience!
- Know the "story" of your food. Where has it come

from? What does it contain? Has it been treated or grown well?

- Break the negative associations that you may have with food. For example if you know that eating when you watch television triggers you to overeat or binge then make it your personal rule that you don't eat whilst you watch TV. Interestingly, when we watch TV we are more likely to eat more than we truly want as our focus is distracted away from the food. Also, whenever you watch TV that is upsetting or violent you are also consuming those feelings with every mouthful you eat. Stop eating fear, anxiety, uncertainty, sadness, struggle or war. Turn the television off! Make a sacred space for you to fully nurture your mind body and soul by eating food that is in alignment with the highest, best, most happiest version of you and connects you to your new "story" and your authentic self.
- Listen to *your* body – not the "experts." Every single "food" or nutrition expert will have their own opinion about what you should or shouldn't be eating. However, the real expert is you and more significantly your incredible body. We are all uniquely biochemically different. How we utilise and process the food we eat depends on many factors including our thoughts, stress levels, metabolism, hormones, movement, energy expenditure, time of day and the relationship with ourselves and the food. Also, no two days will be the same when it comes to eating and nourishing ourselves because we are different in every day and in every moment of our lives. When you try to follow a prescribed eating regime that doesn't take into account the insights of your body, you have stopped listening to the whispers of your body

wisdom. A dear friend of mine went on an all juice diet for three months believing that if she did this then all of her health issues would clear up. However, after the first month she felt worse and by the end of three months her hair had started to fall out and her energy was zero. She felt dreadful. She had put all of her faith and trust in a respected and well known food expert, however she had ignored the feedback that her body was giving her daily. By all means listen to advice and new research but then step back a little and test out if it feels right for you. Evaluate what you hear and listen to your gut. Experiment with different foods and be open to how your body responds. Note if you feel tired or exhausted after eating or if the food enlivens you and makes you feel full of energy and vitality. The old paradigm of following prescribed diets or eating plans perpetuates the old conditioning whereby you put your trust and faith into what someone else is telling you rather than following your own unique path to healing, love and wisdom.

- Make sure that what you desire to eat also desires you! Although you may love a certain food, the food also has to love you back. If what you are eating upsets your body, gives you pain or discomfort or saps your energy levels then this is not love. At the best it's unrequited love but as such will only ever be one sided. Romancing your body means that you eat what you love and that your body loves what you eat. There is no point in choosing something to eat that you love but that has a negative impact That only leads to a toxic relationship and is ultimately unsustainable.

How to eat Chocolate…

Unwrap slowly

Anticipate the pleasure
Open your mouth and say "YES"
Taste it
Really taste it
Let it melt and fill every part of your mouth
Revel in the experience
Be fully present for its deliciousness
Moan a little with pleasure as the taste deepens
Feel the joy
Delight in the sweetness
Swallow the splendour
Taste every last piece
Let it bathe every cell with love
Let the experience bring harmony, pleasure, peace and enjoyment to every part of your being
And when the moment is over...move on, giving thanks that you had it.
This also applies to how to live your life!

6

ROMANCE YOUR BODY WITH YOUR WORDS

To the Incredible You

I know you know this but just a gentle reminder...You can't put yourself down and be who you desire to be in the world at the same time!

(It's all about alignment – Align with LOVING ME!)

Your loving Body! x

When was the last time you whispered "sweet somethings" to yourself? How often do you praise and speak happily about the majesty and beauty of YOU? How much is your inner self dialogue loving, supportive, encouraging, compassionate and uplifting? Words shape and mould us. The words we habitually *listen to* and the words that we habitually *speak* in our life. Words are powerful beyond measure and are perhaps one of the most magnificent and compelling ways to transform our lives and the lives of those around us. When you speak with intention and conscious awareness of what you desire to manifest in your life, your words create an energy that flows within you and around you. This energy is an energetic signature of you, a frequency that is broadcast out into the Universe signalling what you want. The words you use create an imagery within the mind that in turn creates a feeling and a physical response within your body. The old saying, "sticks and stones may break my bones but words will never hurt me" is wrong. Words have the power to wound and destroy or to heal, delight, encourage and inspire you to move mountains. The pen is indeed far mightier than the sword. When it comes to romancing and really loving your body, words are the matchmakers of the soul. When you speak in loving, supportive and appreciative ways about your body, your life opens up millions of connective pathways and possibilities both within you and around you. In ancient times one of the most powerful words ever to be spoken was thought to be the words "I AM" The words that you choose to follow this statement directly begin the creation of what you have just said. So when you say I am tired, I am fat, I am unlovable, I am ugly, I am not good enough, I am too old, I am too stupid, I am not worthy, I am a failure etc you are using your words to craft a destiny that reflects and aligns directly with the words you have chosen to say about yourself. When you stand in front of the mirror and judge yourself harshly you are simply creating more judgement about yourself and your body. How can you ever fall in love with you whilst you are being critical of you? Your words cannot align with the truth of who you are. And as such you will continually attract the experiences, people and events of your life that mirror the words you speak, the thoughts you think and the emotions that you repeatedly experience.

In our early life we are so often repeatedly told what we are *not* by others. We learn what it means to be a part of the family we are born into by what we are *told* about who we are. We are conditioned to accept these beliefs as truths. We learn to create a mindset that becomes a library of "I am nots!" As a schoolchild, whenever we received a report card that said we were less than what was expected we filed that away as the truth. Wherever we were compared to others in a negative way we became less than them. Whenever we judged ourselves by the standards of beauty or the body culture of the day we became not good enough, pretty enough, thin enough, curvy enough or talented enough. However the real truth is that wherever there was a "not" there was a lie! The truth is that from the moment you were born you were (and are) the most magnificent precious beautiful being that has ever existed on this earth. The truth is that you are loved, needed and adored by the Universe and that you are perfect as you are, no matter how you are! When you trace our evolution back to the very first moments of what scientists call poetically the Cosmic dawn you realise the astounding and magnificent truth of how this planet and the life on it came into being. As the first stars sparkled into brilliance and shone their light into the vast empty fog of darkness you realise that these stars were the earliest ancestors of your being. As National Geographic Magazine states, *"When the universe started, there was just hydrogen and a little helium and very little of anything else. Helium is not in our bodies. Hydrogen is, but that's not the bulk of our weight. Stars are like nuclear reactors. They take a fuel and convert it to something else. Hydrogen is formed into helium, and helium is built into carbon, nitrogen and oxygen, iron and sulphur—everything we're made of." And that you too are made of the same stuff as the stars!"*

How eternally romantic! What a glorious notion – that we are made up of stars and as Marilyn Monroe once famously said "All we demand is our right to twinkle!"

When you gaze up at the stars on a heavenly night do you stand and criticise their light or the way they sparkle? Do you judge and compare which stars are brighter or which seem more "perfect" to you? I've never heard someone say that one star is better than another. We are just overawed by their brilliance, beauty and magnificence. Everything we are and everything in the Universe and on earth originated from stardust. And indeed that cosmic dust is still falling onto our Earth, continually finding its way into the plants, the soil, the food we eat and our bodies. How extraordinary to think that our bodies are made of remnants of stars and massive explosions in the galaxies. And that this stardust continually floats through us even today. As the stellar winds from a giant star cause interstellar dust to form ripples, the dust falls—which contains oxygen, carbon, iron, nickel, and all the other elements—out there, and eventually some of it finds its way into our bodies. We are directly connected to the universe, rebuilding our bodies over and again over our lifetimes. What if we saw ourselves as the shining stars that we all are? What if we gave ourselves permission to shine and sparkle reflecting our own inimitable brilliance out into the world? What a glorious world this would be. What if you spoke words that sprinkled starlight and shone with conscious loving intention and meaning. What if you chose to see the truth of your being rather than the "story" of your past? The exciting thing is that we all have the power to write a new story for who we are and the person we desire and long to become. We are not trapped by our past or destined to repeat the endless destructive or self limiting behaviours that we once created to help us to survive. There is a saying that a leopard can't change its spots. It's often applied to human beings in a negative context. However, we are not leopards and we can and do change our spots. Indeed every single day your body is changing and recreating itself. When we look in the mirror we often only see our body as an image that is fixed and unchanging. We see with eyes and a mind that only contains the story of our past. What we see is actually an *illusion* of our body. Our vision is distorted as we see a lifetime of criticisms reflected back at us. Years of being told that we were not good enough, pretty enough, clever enough or good enough blurs what we see and we begin to see what we hate. Our image becomes tainted with comparisons made to an older sister, friend or acquaintance and we become sufferers of an insidious disease called body panic. It's a subtle disease but can spread like wildfire and commonly affects women who are between the ages of adolescence and death. However, according to recent research a high percentage of men are also feeling the effects of not feeling good enough. More than four in five men (80.7%) talk in ways that promote anxiety about their body image by referring to perceived flaws and imperfections and staggeringly 38% of men would sacrifice at least a year of their life in exchange for a perfect body!

Re-write your body script

Romancing your body invites you to become a loving and creative wordsmith. What would it be like to only use the words that inspire love, harmony, beauty, joy and passion in your life? What would it feel like to romance your mind body and soul with the words that they have longed to hear all of your life? What would it be like to love your body with words that wrap pure love and gratitude around every cell, fibre, muscle, tendon, ligament and joint of your body? Instead of criticising your belly for being too fat, too wobbly, too skinny and too old, what if you simply rested your hands on your belly and appreciated it exactly as it is right now? What if you spoke kindly to your thighs and told your bum how fabulous it is? The key thing to know is that your body is listening to every single thing you say. Every cell in your body has an intelligence that enables it to "listen" into the environment of your being. One of the greatest and most powerful things you can do is to change how you repeatedly talk to and about your body. Words bind us together. They connect, communicate, express and create. Think of the most articulate and passionate speakers you have heard and notice how their words inspire you to rise up and become involved in what they are communicating. Words and the way we say them carry an energy signature and frequency that ignites imagination, feeling and actions or behaviours. Take a moment and think about the way that you talk to yourself and your body every day of your life. Do you wake up and tell yourself how beautiful you are? Do you praise yourself for even the smallest things that you did well? Do you look in the mirror and tell yourself that you look gorgeous? Do you whisper your dreams out to the winds as you start your day? And when things don't go as you planned or you are upset by something that has happened in your day, do you quietly comfort yourself with words of love and reassurance? Is the script of your life a nightmare novel or a romantic comedy? Is it a blockbusting adventure or a magical fairytale? The thing is that you are the author of your life, your body, your health, your happiness and your deepest fulfilment. If the life story you are living right now doesn't excite, entice or enthral you then pick up your pen and write another one. Write your new story in single daily mini chapters. It's easy. You don't have to know all of the steps or actions to take. It's not your job to work out all of the details. That belongs to the Universe – your co-author. All you have to do is to start by talking about all the things you love, or give you joy. Focus on what you *want*, not what you don't want. Thank your body for all the great things it does for you day after day and then get out of the way! By that I mean don't second guess yourself, or worry about what will happen in the future. The future is created in the present moment with every thought you think and every action you take. Just write and speak the words that bring your new story alive day after day and trust that everything is unfolding perfectly and with divine timing!

Choose a kinder, more positive word

We all react and respond to words in different ways. For instance one person may use a word that another person finds highly emotionally charged. For example, one of my clients used the word disgusting to describe herself. In response I said that I thought this was quite a harsh way to talk about herself. She looked surprised. She had never thought about it before. She was so used to describing herself as being disgusting and it had no weight or intensity for her. However, the word really stood out for me as it felt so unkind and hard. Especially as she was the furthest thing from disgusting that you could see. Every single relationship in our life has begun with words. From the very first moments in our mothers womb we were attuned to the sound of her voice and the tone and energy it carried. Words are the most powerful shapers and creators of our destiny. They provide the gateways or portals through to unlimited landscapes of adventure, love and inner peace.

Choose a new body story

Imagine that you are a blank page and the way that you live today will etch words on to you and create a story for the world to see. What words do you want emblazoned onto your body? What words will you wear today? What words will you exclude from your vocabulary and your life? What words will you wear with pride, love, ease and joy? Imagine your words are like tattoos. What words would you tattoo on your belly, your arms, your thighs, your face, your legs, and your skin? Would you really choose to go around wearing the most unloving and judgemental or critical words on your body for all to see? Words shape you. Every single word that has been spoken about you has had the power to either uplift you or bring you down. Both the positive and the negative words that you have heard and spoken in your life have been a glorious part of your own magnificent story and journey. Even the words that were left unsaid have infused your being and become a subtext of unheard longings, passions, feelings and unspoken dreams. They may never have been acknowledged or spoken but they carry on writing out their destiny and dreams quietly in the background of your body of being. You may hear their lonely call on those long dark nights of the soul when they rush into rescue you and remind you of the truth of who you really are; that you matter, you are loved and you are absolutely good enough and always have been.

Words walk hand in hand with feelings. Words without integrity, meaning, desire, truth or congruence become placid, flaccid empty vessels of nothingness. And we know it. We can sense or "read" when a person is not being congruent or authentic with what they say. Their mouths may be saying one thing but their body, energy and sensed "feeling" speaks another. Words convey feeling, intention, desire and emotion. They have an energy signature – a frequency that wraps itself around our neurons and whispers out a body map of where our story will go and what it will contain. The chapters and terrains of our lives are written every moment of our life by the choices we make, the words we speak, the love we feel and the deepest connections we can experience with others and ourselves.

There is an abundance of words in the world today. We are rich in the millions of words we can choose to craft and shape our lives and experiences with. Indeed, more and more new words are added to the dictionary every year as words spring up from the back streets of creativity and find their way into the mainstream of the moment. Many of these words confuse and challenge our notion of what was and pull us into looking at what *is* in a new way. The traditional understanding of the word "wicked" used to mean something or someone that was evil, sinful, wrong, bad or corrupt. However, it can also mean someone who is playfully mischievous, naughty, rakish, impish, devilish or cheeky. In more recent times it is also used to describe someone or something that is extremely, cool or great! It is always the intention and feeling behind the word that will captivate and communicate its message. So, when you are creating a new life and body script or story for yourself, make sure that the words you use sit well within your skin.

Choose the words that you most want to *hear* and make them rich in content, creation, charisma and celebration. Choose words that open you up to vast galaxies full of possibilities and wonder. Select words that are expansive, unlimited, joyous and full of enormous potential and creativity. And make them sincere. Make them congruent with your desires and your intentions. If your desire is to love your body then speak words of love to your body. If your desire is to be well, healthy and full of vitality then choose the words that embody this. So often what we desire is left out of everything that we speak about. Instead we speak about what we *don't* want or what is wrong with our life, our body or who we are.

A lovely client that I was coaching kept using the words "It's killing me" to describe how she felt about what was happening in her life. I asked her if she was aware that she had said this five times during our conversation. She shook her head and said she hadn't. I asked her if the things that upset her really *were* killing her. She said "No" As part of our work together I asked her to become really aware and conscious of the words she used and to use words that more accurately described what she wanted to achieve. She nodded and agreed to drop the words "It's killing me". She began to say things like, "It's teaching me". This was also her greatest truth. Everything she had experienced or was experiencing in her life *was* teaching her. She was learning how to become better at communicating her needs, looking after herself, being lovingly assertive with others and ultimately moving past her own limited or rigid patterns of behaviour and beliefs. Just by changing the words she used, she gently gave herself permission to step into more of her personal power and authenticity. She began to say things like "I *get* to do this... instead of I *have* to do this." She started to say, "I *prefer*.... Instead of I *must!*" She began to really open up her vocabulary to stop judging any person or situation (including herself). Instead of jumping reactively on something that someone had said, she began to move into a more neutral position. She said things like, "That's an interesting concept" or "I haven't looked at it that way before." She was able to move more into the questions rather than the answers and found herself saying things like, "What makes you think that?" It was a huge change in her life because as she stopped fuelling her emotions with highly charged words or opinions she created more spaciousness within her mind and body. Her mind couldn't react in the same old way because the emotive triggers and thoughts weren't being activated. When you apply this to romancing your body and loving ALL of who you are, the results are simply extraordinary! Imagine that you look in the mirror and are aware of an old triggering unkind thought that passes through your mind. However, instead of believing it to be true and immediately feeling upset or not good enough, you are able to simply notice it and say, "That's an interesting belief." What happens to the thought? The first thing you may notice is that it loses its power instantly, because there is no emotional charge to feed it. The other amazing thing that you notice is that you are *not* your thoughts. You are the *chooser* of your thoughts! This is exciting because it means that you have the power and option to decide what thoughts you will embody and use to support and love you and what you will simply discard.

Words are thoughts with pictures

Every word conjures up a picture in your mind. Every picture activates an emotion. Every emotion relates to a stored memory. Every memory tells a story and every story shapes your destiny. When you begin to consciously choose words that conjure up the happiest, most loving and beautiful images, you begin to become the true storyteller of your life and your journey. Advertisers know only too well how powerful words are and how highly they can influence us. Just take the following example. Imagine you are out at a restaurant. Which would you rather have? "Oak smoked salmon served in a delicate lemon & parsley sauce" or "dead fish?" The way you describe or talk about anything in your life becomes the *experience* of your life. People often say how miserable the weather is when it's raining. In truth, it's not miserable at all – its just rain, however the word *miserable* will influence you to feel low, depressed or indeed miserable. Words have the power to captivate and influence our human emotions. Someone says the "wrong" thing and we fly off the handle in anger. Another talks to us gently and kindly and we blossom like a flower. Words make us laugh, cry, rejoice, despair, rise to the challenge or give us hope. They can galvanise us into action or defeat us before we've even started. Many people spend their entire lives in search of words of acknowledgment or praise from another human being. A good friend of mine constantly craved her parents to say that they loved her. The words never came. Not because they didn't love her or care about her, but simply because they didn't know how to say the words "I love you" They had never been told that *they* were loved and simply had no point of reference. They couldn't give what they didn't have. And whilst we can't make others tell us we're beautiful, loved, fabulous or special, we CAN choose to tell this to ourselves. And indeed we must, if we are to live out the wonderful life story that is waiting for us to write! Happiness is not dependent on another person telling us how well we've done or how gorgeous we are. Happiness, (as the saying goes) is an inside job! It's up to us to look kindly and lovingly at the decisions and choices we make. It's up to each and every one of us to reach inside our own hearts and tenderly see how beautiful, magical and divine we really are. No matter what may be happening in your life, you have the power to transform it with how you speak about the situation. You can create a catastrophe or calmness. You can cope or you can cave in. Your thoughts and words will influence how you feel and therefore how you choose to act and behave.

Whose story is it anyway?

As I have mentioned before, the stories, beliefs, opinions and judgements that we hold about ourselves have been given to us and handed down through the generations of our family, culture and beliefs about the world. One beautiful way to bring yourself back to being the creator of your story is to ask yourself, *"Who does this thought, opinion or belief belong to?"* Very often you will find yourself remembering that one of your parents always criticised you in this way or perhaps it was a teacher that habitually told you certain things about what you could or couldn't do or achieve. Again, this is powerful because it can help you to put a little distance between *reacting* as if this was the truth about you and seeing it for what it is – a fable, a myth and an old way of perceiving the world that does not belong to you. Thank the thought or belief and say to yourself, "This does not belong to me – it is not mine." I often say quietly to myself, "Delete and uncreate this story". I will then say out loud what it is I desire to create and the truth of who I really am. The question to ask yourself is always, *"What story are you creating and telling with the words you choose?"* When you become mindful of the kind of things you tell yourself (and others) every day, you also put yourself in the best possible position to create what you truly desire.

Use words that make you shine

It is our inner self-talk that is at the heart of any transformational change that we make in our lives. Other people may tell you how beautiful, creative, talented or lovely you are, but it is what *you* say that really holds the master key. This is why developing the most loving relationship with you is truly the gateway to inspired living, fabulous health and inner peace. When the words that you use about yourself are positive, enhancing, loving, kind and uplifting then you send a very clear message to those around you that this is the way that you *choose* and *prefer* to be seen. Words are the magic ingredients in the recipe of life. They ask you to think about what it is you desire to create. You cannot build a loving relationship with words that criticise, harm or put down. You cannot foster trust with empty words that have no integrity or sincerity. However, a word that is spoken with care, thought and awareness has the ability to bring joy, hope, love and positive change to the person who receives it. When this person is YOU – that's when you begin to shine out loud!

Even as you read the words on this page, they are becoming a part of you. As your eyes drink the words in, the meaning and intention behind them is infused into your innermost being. Once read, your mind cannot forget them. They have already imprinted on your soul. They have already changed something within you. You may have felt a subtle shift in your energy already from reading this book. You may become aware of a positive difference in a week, a month or even a year. The words we use are like the sweetest seeds of desire. Within them they hold the greatest creative powerful blueprint of what is to come. Just as you select certain seeds to grow into the desired flowers you want, so too can you sow the seeds of your life with the words you speak.

Honour your word

When we give someone our word, we make a promise: a commitment for something we will do or how we will be. Giving your word is one of the most powerful things you can do because it means so much. Every contract we enter into is based on an agreement with what has been written or said. Every marriage ceremony holds the vows as sacred and binding. Our words matter. Don Miguel Ruiz in his book "The four agreements" cites one of the agreements as "Be impeccable with your word". When you are impeccable with your word you don't use the word against yourself in judging, criticising or shaming. You also don't use it against others in gossiping, blaming or putting someone down. Being impeccable with your word also means that you honour your commitments. You only say that you will do something if you *actually* plan on following this through. Too much sadness is created when we don't honour our word – either to ourselves or to another. In every broken promise there is a loss of trust and a doubt that lodges in our hearts. When we break our word over and over again, we lose faith in ourselves. We begin to doubt our own commitment. Others also begin to wonder if we will really be there for them. One of my own personal breakthroughs was when I decided to stop making empty promises to myself. I had spent what seemed a lifetime in making a promise that I would start that diet tomorrow and this time I would really "be good!" After thousands of "good" Monday mornings and "terrible" Monday evenings I decided that I would stop saying that I was going to diet. I simply didn't believe a word I said anymore and it seemed futile to continue with this painful charade. I felt a sense of relief. And although I hadn't lost any weight, I felt suddenly lighter than I had in years. I began to make my word count. I decided that I would only give my word if I absolutely planned on keeping it. If I didn't know I could keep it then I didn't give my word. I practice this today and it has served me well. Unless I know instantly whether or not I want to do something, I usually take some time in thinking about it before giving an answer. In the old days, I gave my word to everyone and anyone because I wanted to please them. I wanted to be liked and thought well of. The irony of this is that I would often try to find ways to get out of something I had said I would do but didn't really want to. Instead of making people happy, I had achieved exactly the opposite especially if they had been relying on me! It doesn't work on any level. The courage to speak your truth is at the core of keeping your word and in terms of romancing your body it's the very heart of the relationship you have with yourself!

Your word educates others!

A good friend of mine always went out of her way to please her family. They lived close to her and could always tell when she was at home and would call round immediately they spotted her car in the drive. One particular day her two sisters came round and asked her to go walking with them. My friend didn't want to. She had just got in from work. She was tired, exhausted and had been through a difficult day. All she really wanted to do was to kick off her shoes, get into her pyjamas and snuggle in on the sofa with a good film and a cup of hot chocolate. However her sisters were insistent that she come out with them. They kept on at her, cajoling her and insisting that she would feel so much better if she went for a walk. My friend tried to say no. In fact she did really well and managed to refuse their demands for forty minutes! Until they played the high emotional persuasion card that they knew would break down any resolve she might have had. Her oldest sister shrugged her shoulders and looked really sad and disappointed as she said, "Okay, well if you won't go for a walk with us then I won't bother going either." Her other sister also agreed and they turned to leave her house looking crest fallen. That was it! My friend couldn't bear them not to be happy and go for the walk that they were clearly wanting to do so she sighed deeply, picked up her front door keys and headed out of the house with them. The problem with this situation is threefold.

1. My friend educated her sisters that they have to push and push her until she gives in. She taught them quite clearly that "No" actually means that they need to keep digging at her for at least forty minutes until she succumbs to what they want.
2. The walk wasn't done with a genuine, loving intention and desire. My friend said that all through the walk

she felt resentful and angry that she had once again given into doing something someone else wanted. She tried not to be cross with her sisters and tried to make it okay as they walked but inside she carried a resentment that was palpable in the energy around them. She didn't enjoy the warm summer evening; she barely noticed the richness of the flowers in the fields around them or the soft summer rain as it sparkled on her skin. How could she? She wasn't really there. She was stuck in a world of pleasing her sisters and the feelings of angst that this brought up within herself. She loved her sisters dearly and would do anything to make them happy. Unfortunately her behaviour made *her* extremely unhappy in the process.

3. She broke her word to herself and let herself down. Once back home she found herself heading for the bottle of wine she had chilling in the fridge and immediately downed half of it. And so, an old story was once again ignited as she reached for comfort in alcohol, rather than reaching for and communicating her authentic truth.

It's wonderful to do things for others and give your time, energy and love. However, if you do something to make someone else feel happy but it comes at a cost to your own happiness or integrity then that doesn't honour you or them. The other key factor is that the person you are trying to please also knows on some level that you don't really *want* to be there. We can sense when someone really doesn't want to be with us. We feel their energy! So, not only do we cheat ourself by ignoring our own needs, we cheat the other person by not being our authentic self.

How to romance your body with words

- **Begin the day with the word "Thank you!"** Your body has kept you safe all night. A new day is ahead of you. Starting the day with an attitude of gratitude sets the intention for all that is to come. Being alive is a privilege and a gift. You get to have another moment, another chance and a new opportunity to change and fall in love with the wonder that is your life.
- **Refuse to give your word unless you mean to commit to it!** This includes to yourself as well as others! Actually it's especially important to you! If you promise your body that you will give it the most beautiful walk and a beautiful luxurious aromatherapy bath afterwards – keep your word! Every cell in your body hears what you say and anticipates the promised joy and love in your words. Your body will be looking for the walk and the pampering bath. If it doesn't get it, there is a level of trust that has been broken. Imagine how you'd feel if your loved one promised you a romantic meal followed by your favourite show at the theatre and they simply forgot or didn't do it. Only ever break your word to yourself (and others) if there is a really good reason why you couldn't be there or do what you had planned. Tell your body how sorry you are and that you know how disappointed it must be feeling. Thank your body for understanding and reassure it that it is loved.
- **Forgive yourself and move on!** Love is fluid, free flowing, expansive and expressive. Whenever we try to contain our love it finds every single way it can to push through our barriers and rise to the surface. Just as the

flower will find a way through the concrete pavement to blossom fully in the cracks in between! Love will always find a way – if we allow it! The key words here are *"If we allow it"* One of the ways that we stop ourselves from feeling love (either our own or someone else's) is by mentally beating ourselves up or being too harsh on ourselves. This is particularly true whenever we feel that we have made a mistake, let someone down, didn't do our best or haven't achieved what we said we would do. Give yourself a break! Fall back into your own loving arms and allow yourself to be fully received by you! You're okay. There's nothing wrong with you! You're not broken, bad or barmy! You're just a beautiful, fragile, imperfectly perfect human being who is finding your way through your life one moment at a time. It's all too easy to abandon ourselves when we feel that we have failed or disappointed in some way. However, this is when you need YOU the most! Learn from what happened, forgive yourself and move on!

- **Raise your vibration with your words**! Spiritual teachers, Shamans and Esoteric thought leaders have known for a long time the effect that words can have on our body and mind. They have taught that our body is programmable by language, words and thought. Russian scientists have backed this up and have shown that our DNA can actually be reprogrammed by words and certain frequencies. This is an extraordinary development in the field of mind body medicine. In terms of romancing your body, it is a powerful and transformational piece of how to truly live your best life! The more conscious you become in terms of what you are saying and how you are saying it, the more you are able to shift your own energy frequency into a higher state of being! This in turn attracts more of the "good stuff" that you desire in your life.

- **Choose your words consciously!** What would you choose to say if you only had a thousand words left to say? There is an Eddie Murphy film called A thousand words. In the movie, Eddie's character tries to sign a deal with a spiritual guru. He fakes meditation and enlightenment in order to get an audience with the great man. However, little did he know that he was about to encounter his biggest test – a Bodhi tree appeared in his backyard representing his very life. The leaves on the branches represent his words. Every time he spoke a word or wrote a word, a leaf falls off the tree. When all the leaves have fallen off, he dies along with the tree. Imagine that you only had a thousand words left – what would you say? Who would you speak to and what would you tell them? How would you speak to yourself? What really matters for you to say and what can be left unsaid? It's a good exercise to do as it really makes you mindful of what is truly important in your life and how meticulous you need to be with the words you speak. Sometimes words aren't necessary. There is nothing we can say – we can only be there with our presence and our feelings. There is so much "noise" in our lives from the endless TV, news, gossip, mobile phones, magazine or newspaper articles, music, advertising etc. Becoming aware of your words helps to put a space between your thoughts and what comes out of your mouth. You begin to quiet the noise and begin to choose more clearly what you want to create and communicate. It is here that you can become aware of the words you don't say.

Ask yourself the following questions:

1. What is the sound of your soul?
2. What words have you longed to utter but have kept yourself in silence?
3. Where have you withdrawn your words from other people? Is there something you have left unsaid?
4. What words do you speak only to yourself and are they what you long to hear?
5. When do you need to hold your tongue?
6. When do you need to speak out loud?
7. If you only had a few words left to say, how would you make them count? Who would you say them to, why and when?

These simple questions can be really helpful in understanding what truly matters in your life. If you only had a few words left to say, how would you make it count? Who would you say them to and when?

- **Say sorry to your body!** This one is so underestimated and so vitally important for building the most loving relationship with your body. So often in our lives we treat our body as if it's simply not there or has no feelings. If we did this to anyone else they would walk away from us in an instant. However, when it's our body, it seems as if we think we can get away with being rude, disrespectful and simply uncaring. For example, if your partner or best friend stubbed their toe on the floor or banged their elbow hard, you would most probably be sympathetic. At the very least you might say, "I'm so sorry you hurt – that must have been painful!" Have you ever said that to *you* when you have stubbed your toe or banged your elbow? Most often we just let out an expletive and hobble around for a while cursing the door or how stupid we are for not looking where we were going! The next time any part of your body hurts, try being there for it. Slow down, take some time to put your hand over the tender area and tell your body how sorry you are that it is in pain. Notice where your body hurts and be there with it. It's such a simple loving thing to do and yet we rarely give ourselves the time of day when it comes to looking after our own needs, pains and pleasures. Once again this is usually because we weren't taught how to do this when we were little. Well meaning parents may have tried to minimise our hurt or distress to try and take the pain away from us. They may have said things like, "There, there don't be silly, it's only a little bump!" Or "don't be a cry baby, come on, it's nothing!" Our pain needs to be validated along with our feelings. All an emotion ever wants to do is to be expressed, felt and then released. If we are forever shutting down what we feel or minimising a painful situation, we may begin to lose touch with our true emotions and sensitivity. One of my clients told me how whenever she was hurt or upset, her mother would always tell her that it was nothing and she was being silly for being upset. Her mother meant well, however, the impact of this was that my client always doubted what she *truly* felt about things. Whenever she had to make a decision in her life she always sought everyone else's opinion about what was the right thing to do. When it came to relationships, she never knew if what she was feeling was real. In any argument she had with people she always blamed herself because she never really knew if she had a *right* to feel what she felt. She continually made her self wrong because she doubted if what she was feeling was right!

- **Speak about what you WANT** – not what you don't want! It's simple but not necessarily easy to do this one! People are often so much more in touch with what they don't want or what makes them unhappy. When I ask someone what they want, they will often pause, look a bit confused and say that they don't really know or they're not quite sure. However, if I ask them what they don't want, they can give me a list as long as my arm! We've been trained to focus on what's not right or what doesn't work. We've been primed to look for the negative instead of the positive. When you catch yourself talking about what you *don't* want, stop, take a breath, refocus and begin again by talking about what you DO want. Easy ways to do this are to begin sentences with the words, "I wish, I prefer, I love, I can't wait until…I'm excited by…I'm happy about…I'm so blessed to…I would like it if….One of my dreams is…etc.
- **Change the word "BUT" to "AND"** This is a simple and very effective technique that helps you to widen your dreams and keep your power in the present moment of creation and elation! Very often people will tell you what they would love to do and then they put the word "But" into the sentence which completely negates what they have just said. For example, "I'd love to write a book BUT I haven't got the time" Or, "I'd really enjoy going on that course BUT I'm probably too old to start something like that!" Everything after the word "but" stops the energy and the desire, because we have just given a good reason why it won't happen. So, use the word "And" and

watch how you instantly give yourself permission for your dreams to become possible. For example, "I'd love to write a book AND I'm going to jot a few ideas down today" Or, "I'd really enjoy going on that course AND I'm going to find out when it starts."

- **Tell you that you LOVE YOU!** People in love constantly affirm the love that they are feeling. They want the world to know that they are happy. They want to shout it from the rooftops that they have found this thing called love and they are ecstatic about it! They want their beloved to feel loved, safe, special and secure. So, tell yourself that you love you. Speak highly of YOU. Use words that caress your soul and wrap you up in love and light. Don't take it for granted that you know that you love you – say it! And say it again and again! Repetition is a powerful tool when it comes to reshaping our lives and creating health, happiness and wellbeing. Even if you don't feel that you love you right now – just simply decide to *choose* love! You don't have to believe it right at this moment, you simply have to choose it! Just the fact that you are reading this book means that there is a *desire* to love your body and fall in love with your life. So choose LOVE! Choose it again and again.
- **Increase your vocabulary of fabulous words.** Select one word from the list below every day and make it your goal to use it as often as possible throughout your day.
- Fabulous... Invincible... Wonderful...Raring to go... Exciting... Empowered...Brilliant...Gifted...Alive... Awesome...Amazing...... Sumptuous...Just perfect... Centered...Really happy...Over the moon Terrific... Grateful...Energised...Couldn't be better... Outrageous...Blessed...Superb...Vivacious...

Unstoppable...Vibrant...Beautiful... Unshakeable... Exuberant...Ecstatic...Spectacular...Sensational... Magical...Extraordinary...Inspired...Motivated... Passionate... Enthusiastic...Exhilarated...Incredible... Monumental...Phenomenal....Confident... Captivated...Excellent...Fantastic...Great...Gorgeous...

- Enraptured...Blissful...Tremendous...Dynamic... Luminous...Soulful...Spirited....Joyful... Uplifted....Loved...Effervescent...Sunlit...Unlimited... Eternal...Cosmic...Fascinating...Magnificent... Marvellous...Splendid...Dazzling...Stunning... Grand...Bewitching...Exquisite...Majestic...Radiant... Sublime...Excellent...Divine... Adorable...Glamourous...
- Magnetic...Mesmerising...Tantalising...Breathtaking... Enchanting...Scrumptious...Delightful...Delicious... First class...Fantastic...Stupendous....Legendary...Out of this world....On cloud nine...Wild...Free... Miraculous...Impressive...Heart-stirringingly beautiful...Thrilling...Exceptional... Special....Glorious...Epic...Serene...Gleeful...Full of radiant health...Playful...Elated....In seventh heaven... Tickled pink...Blithe...Flying high...Sparkling... Shining...Heavenly...Frolicsome...Ebullient...Zestful... Rosy...Blossoming....Buoyant...Expansive... Invigorated...Carefree...Sunny...Easy Breezy... Fortunate...Rich...Snug as a bug in a rug...Content... Harmonious...Glowing...Bouncy...Starry...Kittenish... Bright...Flourishing...Golden....Positively balmy... Priceless...Unique...Resplendent.... Enthralling....Magnetic...Yummy...Delectable... Flowing...Elegant...Impressive...Riveting... Luxurious...Sumptuous...Glossy...Opulent...Simply the best!

Can you just imagine speaking about yourself with some of these fantabulous words. Imagine being asked how you are and instead of uttering the usual, "Not so bad," or "Can't complain" you answer with "I'm just glorious today!" or even, "I'm feeling Spectacular and Adorable!" Even if you weren't feeling that way, it would make you smile just by answering with those words. The amazing thing is that when you say something that isn't in the usual run of what people say, it wakes them up and YOU! Changing our old behaviour patterns and habits is about doing something different. We need to shake up the old ways of thinking, doing, being and behaving. Words are a wonderful way to achieve this because they are the blueprint of your soul's desires. We create with our words. Words are the architects of the body and shapers of the mind. What we speak about, comes about. Be mindful of the words you are using because they are shaping your thoughts, your experiences, your body, your happiness, vitality and your destiny.

7

ROMANCE YOUR BODY WITH MOVEMENT

Movement never lies. It is a barometer telling the state of the soul's weather to all who can read it – Martha Graham

To move is to be alive. Everything in the entire Universe is always moving, expanding and contracting. Everything in our life begins with movement. Even when you are sitting still, your entire body is moving gently. Your breathing continues, rising and falling. Your heart beats out its steady rhythm, your blood flows, your thoughts fire their neural pathways, your nails keep growing, your stomach carries on digesting, your ears keep picking up the sound signals all around you. Your cells are always either building up and regenerating or breaking down and being swept away. Your body is always in a continual state of expansion and contraction, ebb and flow, protection (fear) or growth (love). We trust our body to carry out these processes without having to actively "DO" anything about them. We don't have to tell ourselves to breathe – we just inhale and exhale naturally. You don't have to force your heart to beat – it just does. Our body simply knows how to be the best body it can be. And, if we allow our body to experience and communicate its wisdom to us we are able to tap into the subtle energy messages and clues it sends us about how we are living our life, what our body needs to heal, feel powerful, strong and flexible and to thrive in the most joyful state imaginable. Unfortunately most people have no idea of how GOOD their body can feel. We are so used to dumbing down the innate wisdom and energy of our body that we have lost touch with what it means to feel fabulously ALIVE, healthy & well! Movement (and especially conscious movement) can help bring back that sense of aliveness, joy, vitality and wellbeing. It can help us to connect to our inner knowing and free up old hurts, patterns, habits and beliefs.

Meaningful movement

Every movement we make in our lives has meaning. Even without our realising it we are continually expressing our deepest thoughts, beliefs and core qualities with every movement we make. We may say one thing with our words but our body will always speak the truth of what we *really* feel and believe to be true. Indeed only 7% of communication is actually through the words we speak. The rest is through our facial expressions and body language.

Our body also is the quickest way to alert us to when we are resisting or creating struggle in our life. Every single response in our body has a direct and specific meaning and message. When your shoulders rise in tension or you find yourself grinding your jaw, or clenching your stomach, your body is giving you clear signs that there is a sense of unease, resistance, pain or unhelpful thoughts at play. However, because so much of the time we are living in our heads, we often disregard or fail to notice these subtle energetic clues of dis-ease from our body. When you become more mindful and aware of the movements and messages your body is giving you there is an opportunity for you to consciously drop into a more relaxed, open and heart centred way of being in (and with) your body. As you become more engaged and present in your body, you are also able to communicate with your body in a way that will be readily understood and accepted by your body.

When the way that you speak aligns with the way you move, feel and engage in your life you are living in your greatest wisdom and authenticity. Our body reflects and mirrors all that we are and all that we have ever been. It is the container and the story keeper of the past and also the doorway to our best and brightest future. It is also the messenger of the moment as it is continually "speaking" to us in the forms of feelings, insights, sensations and "textures" (lightness, heaviness, expansive, contracted, cold, warm, dense, roughness, fluidity and rigidity). We are continually shaping and reshaping our body every minute of every day by the thoughts we think, the foods we eat, the way we move, the qualities we embody, the perceptions we hold and how we actually engage and inhabit the present moment – the degree to which we are fully present, available, conscious and aware. Our body is also reflecting and communicating back to us the journey of our life as it unfolds in every single moment. This is exciting because we now have the ability to speak to our body in a way that it will readily understand and will also respond to. This also plays a huge part in how we think about exercise and moving our body. When you begin to understand that every single movement you make in your life has meaning, intention and purpose, the old fitness paradigm shifts completely. Traditional fitness regimes mainly focussed on the body. It was all about being the fittest that you could be or about looking a certain way. Much of the movements were linear with emphasis on repetition until you fatigued a specific muscle. The focus was on push, force or resistance. In the eighties we were instructed to feel the burn. We were told that if there was no pain there was no gain! Many of the group exercise classes were about pushing the body to the limit in the shortest amount of time. Even the more recent popular high intensity interval training classes focus on pushing yourself to the hardest, highest and fastest you can endure for short moments of time. The abbreviation of High Intensity Interval Training stands for HIIT! Why do we desire to hit our body into shape! Ask yourself *how* do you desire to *feel* within your body? When you push your body hard, your body receives the message that it has to be pushed and pushing becomes one of your body drivers or beliefs. When we force ourselves to go beyond what feels good, the body anchors in the energy of force and applies this to all areas of your life. For example, back in the eighties when I was teaching around 27 workout classes a week I was also around a size 24. Whilst I had learned to love my shape and size and felt fit and healthy at this size my body refused to lose any weight at all. It didn't matter what I ate or didn't eat or how much exercise I did – my body remained pretty much the same. I remember one TV presenter saying to me when I showed up to teach the morning workout on GMTV, "It's amazing that you do all this exercise and yet you're still so heavy." What I now understand is that all of the exercise that I did was performed with the following 'drivers' or body beliefs as motivators. I believed that I had to work really hard and long to lose any weight at all. I believed that my body wouldn't change shape unless I sweated it out in the gym at least three hours a day. I believed that if my muscles didn't hurt after a class, then I hadn't really worked out properly and that I had to lift heavier weights in order to see any progress at all. I bought into the idea that I had to whip my body into shape as if my body were some unruly and wild creature that had to be tamed and caged. Interestingly this was also how I lived much of my life. I forced myself to do things that I didn't really want to do. I pushed myself to keep going with projects even though I was exhausted. I stayed up too late and only felt that I was succeeding if I was struggling and forcing myself to achieve. I also felt guilty if I sat down for a moment or wasn't engaged in doing something that I thought was productive. The only times that I managed to slide out of this syndrome was when I had overeaten or binged, which gave me the opportunity to escape for just a little while.

When I compare this approach to the woman that I am today, I am stunned by my own personal transformation in which the only movement I did was gentle walking and soft, healing energy medicine exercises, (Chakranetics™). Combined with conscious authentic eating and mindful movement my weight happily released from my body, my joints stopped hurting and my energy and vitality soared. Ultimately, we have to ask ourselves what we really want from our movement programmes and how we desire to *feel* within our beautiful body. Apart from the very high-end elite athletes most people simply want to feel healthy, strong, flexible, happy and free in their body. We want to be able to walk with ease, to stretch and reach, to twist and turn easily and to be strong enough to carry our own body weight with flow, grace and fluidity. We want to be able to play with our children, dance, curl up on the sofa, and get up and down from the floor or chairs easily and to engage in all of life's delights. When you are in pain or can't walk very far because you're too tired or your joints hurt, then these simple joys and pleasures disappear from your life. As we head into our older years, moving with ease and freedom is key to staying youthful and independent. It is the ultimate body commodity that we all desire.

The body speaks your story

The body speaks quite literally and is always telling and retelling our story right from before we were born. Everything that we have experienced from our earliest moments are stored and felt within our body. When we were shouted at, our muscles contracted and our stomachs tensed and knotted up in upset. When we laughed we rolled over, kicked our legs in the air and threw back our heads, letting our body gulp huge amounts of air.

The stories others told us also became part of our early body beliefs and memory patterns. For example, if we were told we were too tall we may have allowed our shoulders to round over and let our back bow outwards as we tried to appear smaller in height. Our breathing may have become shallow as we compressed our chest and our eyes may be permanently down-cast as we look to the floor instead of the sky. As we continued into adulthood, this posture (created from a belief or story) is now a cause for pain, stress and dis-ease.

The body is your subconscious mind. Everything that you were ever told or experienced becomes part of your biology of belief. Your core beliefs generally originate in childhood and are carried through by the storytellers before you – your parents, grandparents and as far back as time itself. We "wear" these core beliefs (both positive and negative) which are carried energetically in the body through our physical habits. Posture, breathing and energy levels. Essentially the body is a transmitter of the energy you carry through the thoughts you believe.

Unravelling your body story

To understand your own unique body story it is helpful to look at your body with fresh, new and curious eyes. Instead of focussing on what you feel is inadequate or "wrong" ask yourself the following questions instead.

- How does your particular body serve your purpose?
- What is the gift in the form you have taken on?
- What events have shaped your body through good fortune, accident. trauma, genetic lineage, or daily habits?
- What is the message your body sends to the world and to those in your immediate circles?
- What does your body protect?

- What does your body express?
- How does your body love to move?
- What has your body taught you?
- Where have you withdrawn from your body?
- What does your body need the most?
- If your body were a storybook character or mythological being, what would it be?
- Take an inventory of your body. Scan your body and ask yourself what does this curve, this freckle, this scar, this bunion, this wrinkle, this belly, these hips etc tell me about the body of my beliefs.

The amazing thing is that when you *consciously* choose to change your beliefs, perceptions and the way that you move, you create a new body story and therefore a new body reality. One that is based on joy, health, freedom, vitality and well-being. Patterns and habits become locked in the body as stored pieces of information. When you change the way you move you activate and access a new neural and body pathway that can lead to increased conscious awareness, health and vitality. Try this simple exercise for a day and see what happens. Try to open all doors, car doors, cupboards, windows, bags, packaging etc with your non-dominant hand. Notice what happens and how easy or hard it is. Just by doing this simple (but not necessarily easy) exercise, you begin to shake up old patterns and habits that have resided in your body-mind for years. The mind "wakes" up as it tries to adjust to your new ways of doing things and as such you are living more in the moment. It's a great exercise for becoming aware of just how much we do through habit and without being conscious. This principle also applies to your fitness, exercise or movement class. The brain thrives on variety and new ways of experiencing the moment. When you begin to play with movement and find new ways of performing regular tasks or exercises you create more plasticity in your brain. Brain plasticity (from the

Greek word 'plastos' meaning moulded) refers to the extraordinary ability of the brain to modify its own structure and function following changes within the body or in the external environment.

So for example the next time you do a simple bicep curl you may want to experiment with varying the speed and way that you perform it. Try visualising the colour green flooding through the bicep. (Green is associated with the heart chakra which flows down and through into your arms). Visualise drawing towards you something or someone you love dearly as you raise and lower the arm. Flow the feeling of love through your bicep. You may also want to add in a body mantra that says, "My arms are strong, capable and loving and I embrace my life with joy" Feel the movement from the inside out and notice how the whole of your body is engaged and involved with the activity. This way of moving is a fully conscious and mindful experience that brings *all* of you into the moment. It is quite different to the old ways of moving the body which required very little action apart from the physical lifting and lowering of the arm. Indeed, in the old fitness paradigm many class participants could simply carry out doing bicep curls but be thinking of what they were going to have for dinner that evening. Every muscle has a story and every movement the muscle makes changes the next movement. However, the body's story has been neglected from most fitness or exercise regimes. Why does this matter? Because unless you begin to understand that the body is a Universe in microcosm – always expanding, building, merging, contracting, ebbing and flowing, you miss the information that your body has to share with you. Your mind may decide that you need to walk for five miles a day; however, your body may have other ideas. When you are able to begin to read your own body codes and talk back in a language your body understands you may choose to walk just a mile and spend more time stretching instead.

The fastest way to change how you feel is to change how you move!

When you romance your body with movement, you create alchemy in action. There is a flow to your life and your days. The body *loves* to move. It thrives on simply enjoying being its own fullest expression of itself. If you watch a baby move, one of the first things you notice is the freedom in which that baby loves to explore and move their own body. Toes and hands are an endless source of fascination and every single emotion and sensation is expressed fully in the moment as it is experienced. A baby moves with intention and awareness in present time. She or he is embodied in the moment. Young children move with ease and grace. As you watch children grow, their movement is congruent with their feelings. A child may skip along the street in delight and exuberance for living. They love to jump, hop, spin and see the world from upside down angles. They are so full of living that their little body can barely contain all the energy, curiosity and joy they feel. The same is true when they feel sad, angry, upset or fearful. They show it through every part of their body. They haven't yet learned how to hide their true emotions or lock them down into some kind of "accepted normality." They are real, authentic and in the moment. When a child is disappointed, their little face drops in sadness. They wouldn't dream of hiding their feelings behind an assumed smile. When they are happy, their face and body ripples with bubbles of laughter. Their giggles are infectious as their delight is so obvious to share and experience. Their whole body shakes in joy!

As we grow and move through our lives, this spontaneous and authentic movement is often lost or hidden as our conditioned habits and behaviour replace our genuine felt responses. We worry what others might think if we laugh too loud or cry too much. Our body begins to replicate and express our deepest conditioned beliefs and thoughts that we have been told about who we are. When we feel too fat we often unconsciously hold our stomach in for fear of looking too big. When we feel we are too tall, we may stoop over in order so as not too appear too dominating, trying to shrink our body to meet the size, shape and demeanour of the other body's around us. When we feel fearful or unsafe in the world we may begin to take more shallow breaths (or even hold our breath) as we live in fear of what someone else might say about us. The way that our body moves and expresses itself is like a print out or a receipt for what thoughts are being thought and feelings being felt (or not allowed to be felt). When you are in pain it is always a request for some sort of change. Your body is asking you to do something different. The easiest way to make positive changes in your life is to change how you move and change how you think. Each one feeds off and reinforces the other. When you move, your brain has to adapt to it. When you think, your body has to also adapt and change. The interplay between body, emotions, mind and spirit occur in the moment. They are as one unit. The body is always in motion, always listening and responding to your latest thought, belief, emotion or experience. Every thought you have contributes to the ongoing story of your body and is mirrored by what you see, feel and experience. One day you may look younger and revitalised. Another day you may feel exhausted and drained. You may find that some lines or wrinkles fade and disappear and other days you may find that a spot has suddenly appeared with no notice. Our body continually shifts and changes according to what we are thinking and what "story" we are telling ourselves that day. Depending on what your latest sub plot or storyline is, it's as if your body dashes off into the dressing room for a quick change of costume! We wear our body of beliefs as easily as we choose which outfit we shall put on for the day.

Move because you love the feeling it gives you!

I was coaching a beautiful young woman recently who had come to me because she was experiencing a deep sense of dissatisfaction with her body and her life. She was not where she wanted to be. I asked her what she meant by this. She replied that she had spent most of her life chasing an ideal image of her body and how everything would be "perfect" in her life when she had achieved this image. Like so many people she had spent most of her life waiting for it to really begin. She had put her life, dreams and happiness "on hold" whilst she waited for her body to become as she wanted it to be in order for her to go after what she truly desired. The words she used consistently throughout our conversation were, "When I've....lost weight, toned up, slimmed down, I'll start that course, go to that party, move into my own place, start dating etc". She resented other women who seemed to have the "perfect" body and therefore (in her mind), the perfect life. She based her own value or worth on how slim she was compared to her friends. When she was out socially with her friends she would be the one to hold back and go quiet if guys came up to chat to them. In her mind she believed that unless she was thin, she had nothing to offer. Why would the guys go for her when they could be with her skinny friends? As we worked together she began to realise that everything she did was in the pursuit of attaining this mental image of her "perfect" body. She pushed herself hard in workouts. She counted exactly how many calories she had eaten and weighed herself constantly to check her progress. My heart went out to her. I had been through that journey too and the only place it leads to is unhappiness. One of the key things that came out of our discussions was that she actually hated the exercise she was doing. She didn't enjoy it but did it because of how many calories she could burn off in an hour. Her real turnaround came when she tore her calf muscle during a particularly strenuous workout. Her body had been through enough. This was a really challenging time for her as she couldn't exercise any more and every movement she made was full of pain. However, it was also the beginning of a new relationship with her body. Suddenly she had time and space to take stock of what she was doing. As she began a slow process of rehabilitation she was forced to move differently; slower and with more conscious awareness. She went outside for gentle walks and realised that she had never spent time noticing how beautiful the scenery was before. In the past she would have only gone outside to clock up the miles as she trained for the latest marathon. Forget the scenery, she was more interested in her timing and calories burned. She also had to deal with the torrent of negative self talk that suddenly seemed louder than ever before in her head. In the past she had managed to block everything out with her obsessive exercise but now she was being asked to *feel her feelings* and be more aware of the demanding voice of her mind. As her calf muscle slowly healed, so did her mind and spirit. She stopped running away from her beautiful body and began to seek out ways she could enjoy it instead. The biggest change was when she said that she wanted to move in ways that gave her joy and aliveness. She took up dancing, started hill walking and went swimming every few weeks. Her body thrived. She was glowing with energy. A body that is loved radiates happiness.

My soul came here to dance!

When you romance your body with movement you begin to dance with the unlimited flow of the entire Universe. You begin to notice how you move through your days and the energy that flows through and around your limbs. Most of the movements we make are unconscious. Many people have no idea of how they habitually move or what moves them. The body is largely forgotten except when they feel pain or discomfort in an area of the body. Romancing your body with movement is more than taking an exercise class or spending an hour at the gym. It's a way of being and flowing in your body. It's about fully inhabiting and being present in your body every moment in your life. Exercise and movement are two different things and indeed inspire very different reactions. The word exercise can be loaded negatively for many people as they feel that they *should* be fitter or feel guilty because they *ought* to go to a gym more often! Movement on the other hand is something that we all do every day of our lives. Compare the feelings of going out walking in nature on a beautiful warm summers day, because it gives you joy to getting up at six am to burn off three hundred calories before you get to work. One form of movement will be inspiring health and congruency and the other will be tolerating and coping with the demands that is being asked of it. The secret of course is to match your movement to the type of exercise that you love to do. It's quite another matter if your body genuinely adores to be up at six am and doing a hard workout before the sun is even up! It's all about finding ways to move that are congruent with your body and in alignment with your soul. When you choose to move in ways that make your body feel free, alive, lithe, strong, balanced and full of passion, you connect and map out a sacred pathway that your soul remembers. A spiral pathway of pure love and belonging. The soul loves to dance – that's why it chose your beloved body as its dancing partner. When we block this pathway by demanding that the body conforms to the mind's idea of exercise or traditional fitness programs, we lose the essence of inner knowing, vitality and oneness.

If you were to film every single movement that you did in the day from waking up to going to bed you would see a beautifully choreographed dance of your life. You would see your body standing, sitting, lying down, walking, turning, twisting, reaching up, bending low. You would notice your posture and be able to tell exactly what you were feeling or experiencing by the tilt of your head, the line of your spine, the space in your hips and the flow and form of your muscles. Every thought you have is played out in the symphony of your body and resonates throughout your entire being. When you feel unconfident your body shies away from the moment. Even the tilt of the head is pulled back and slightly off to the side. Your eyes may dart back and forth as if you're checking to see if the environment is safe. When you're tired, the body loses length and spaciousness. It folds in on itself, contracts and seeks to curl up or snuggle down. Movements become slower, heavier and feel as if they are weighted in some way. Even your blinking becomes slower and more languid as your eyes seek to close and rest their lashes on the curve of your cheek. Romancing your body with movement means that you begin to become more aware of the daily dance of your body, the shapes it makes, the energy, lightness or heaviness it feels. It invites you to become more fully embodied in every moment of every day.

Alchemy in Action

Action is the mind in motion. The body is the great translator and alchemist of the mind's desires, creativity and longings. Nothing can happen without some kind of corresponding movement in the body. You may have a wonderful idea of a book you want to write. However, without you sitting and actually writing the book, it will always remain an idea. You may know intellectually what to do to change or improve some area of your life but until you actually take action and do it, you do not truly know. Our body turns our ideas, desires and passions into pure gold. When you listen to your heart and use your beautiful mind to amplify the heart's desire, you create a powerful synergy and chemistry that manifests your dreams. It's the formula of knowing plus doing equals being. Mind, body and spirit working together in perfect harmony and synchronicity. I always feel that my heart is the boss and my mind is its fabulous PA (Personal

Assistant). The more that I use my mind to do the bidding of my heart the more aligned, confident, fulfilled and happy I am.

If your body had a choice, what movements would it love to do?

How would your body love to move more? What movements bring you joy, peace, happiness and vitality? The body knows how it loves to move and *when* it wants to move. Sometimes the body is quiet and small, other times the body is enormous with its capacity for expression and vitality. When you demand that your body only exercises or moves in a certain way at a certain time, you miss out on the wisdom and wellness of your cells, muscles, heart and soul. When you force your body to comply with the demands of your mind, you disengage the magnificent personal trainer that lies in every cell of your entire being. The old fitness paradigm was all about shaping up your body, tightening and toning and generally forcing it to comply with the ideal image that you held in your mind of how you desired your body to look. It didn't really matter how your body might *feel* as long as it looked the way you wanted. The old mantra of "no pain, no gain" was paramount here, as people pushed and demanded their body to get into shape – no matter what the cost may be! It seemed acceptable to force, struggle and "whip" the body into shape as if it were some unruly creature that needed to be tamed and "broken" or bullied into submission. The result was a sense of disconnection with the way that people felt and the way that they appeared. I know this only too well in my own journey with learning to love my body. I too demanded that my body should be a certain way. I dreamed and hankered after the "perfect" size ten images that I saw in the magazines around me. I fantasised that my life would be "perfect" if only I could get to that place of body nirvana. However, my body had different ideas. No matter how much I tried to force it to comply with my unrealistic and brutal demands, my body would always show me that it had other ideas. At times my body was able to maintain that six stone weight loss for a few months. However, sooner or later it would assert it's old "story" about what I had been conditioned to believe about my body and who I was and the weight would creep back on. It had no other choice. My body was simply doing its job as it tried to bring me back into alignment with what I had been *conditioned* to feel and believe about my body. At that time my beliefs were that I couldn't love my body until it was thin and that I was unacceptable and unlovable as I was. I saw my body as the reason for all my unhappiness and hated the fact that I had to actually "live in" the body I had. I was ashamed of my body and also myself. I felt that I didn't fit in (literally) and saw my body as a barrier to all that I desired in my life. This had been my "*story*" for as long as I can remember. My poor body was simply doing its best to "act out" and give me what I was thinking about, believing and feeling about myself. At that time in my life, there was no communication between my conscious mind, my soul, my body and me. I didn't want to hear what my body had to say or how it felt. I simply wanted it to shut up and do what I said. Interestingly, I saw this reflected in some of the wonderful women that I taught in my fitness classes every day. We would have the most amazing class – full of fun, laughter and hot, sweaty, tough exercises that would have us gasping for breath and feeling "the burn." And at the end of class, as we packed up to go, many of the ladies would talk about their weight and their body in negative, disparaging ways. One fabulous class participant came up to me at the end of class and lifted up her Lycra sports top to reveal a flat, tanned and toned tummy. "Look at all of that!" she said, trying to pinch together a tiny amount of skin between her fingers. I leaned closer and tried to see what she was showing me. "And," she went on, "Look at the size of my thighs!" Again, I could see nothing wrong with them and asked her what the matter was. She looked at me as if I was mad and said, "How come I'm doing all of this exercise and I still look like this?" I was stunned. To me she looked fabulous! Here was this attractive, fit, intelligent woman who disliked parts of her body to such an extent that she felt miserable and inadequate and embarrassed about a shape many of us would love to have had. She had a body ideal or image in her head that she wanted to achieve and even though she was already slim, toned, fit and beautiful – she simply couldn't see this. And in this gap – this space between what we idealise and crave and where we actually are lays pain, upset and suffering.

Learn how to speak BODY!

When you learn how to speak in your body's language, you begin to connect and "come home" to your authentic true self. A self that has always been present and is eternal in its essence. Your true self has nothing to do with moulding your physical form into some conditioned notion of what shape you should be. It is all about how you truly *feel* about being in the shape that you are in. When we begin to unravel ourselves from the tyranny of the *conditioned body* we begin to flow and form into a new sense of being, wellness, joy and deep inner peace and acceptance. This has been (and is) my own personal journey. A journey home into the deepest parts of me that have ached and longed to be loved and touched with compassion.

As my own body journey unfolded I began to create a very different type of movement practice for myself. I had been suffering with chronic pain for many years. I had crippling arthritis in my knees, fingers, toes and elbows. The high kicks that I loved to do when I was in my twenties seemed a very long time ago and I knew that my body wouldn't be able for the hard workouts I used to enjoy. After being bed bound for months on end I began to search for a new way to move. A way that my body would love and also that my body could do. I began to combine my dance and fitness training with my expertise in psychology, coaching and energy medicine to produce a new mindful movement modality called Chakranetics™. Chakranetics™ is a conversation with your body and also your wildest longings. It is about the movement of your life and how you are moving within your life and within your body. Every practice always invites questions and curiosity. The questions are always based around movement. Where are you moving to and from? What is behind the impulse to move? What is your intention with the movements you make and what do your movements tell you about your feelings, attitudes, beliefs, desires and longings? The focus in Chakranetics™ is always on the feeling and how this feeling informs and forms you.

Move closer to who you truly are!

Chakranetics™ is a body based moving meditation practice - it is also a spiritual experience. It is a beautiful blend of mindfulness, movement medicine and energy psychology. Many spiritual practices are designed to move you away from your body as they ask you to ascend into a higher state of consciousness. Sometimes this can feel as if the body has been forgotten, however, Chakranetics™ moves you more deeply and fully INTO your body. It invites you to descend into your bones, muscles and cells with your full spirit. Your body is where you live, where your soul calls home throughout this lifetime. The aim is to manifest the gentle beautiful whispers of your soul within every part of your body so that you can connect, engage, heal and build a wonderful new and loving relationship with you. Chakranetics™ aligns your soul with the authentic expression of who you truly are. When you embody your personal truth you live from this place of spiritual connection every day of your life. You relax more deeply, live more consciously and enjoy the abundance that life offers.

If you are interested in discovering more about Chakranetics™ then please visit www.chakranetics.com for more information and details of how you can become a Certified Chakranetics™ mindful energy movement teacher.

Engage, embrace, embody!

Movement has been relegated to something that we do in order to achieve a required result. The actual experiencing of the movement and the feelings, awareness, intention and meaning of the movement has been largely forgotten or ignored. Like so many things in life, the focus has been on the end result rather than the journey and process of the embodied moment of movement. I was amused to read recently about a local gym that had kitted out all of their treadmills and stationary cycles with access to the internet and social media. They boasted that you could do your workout and read your emails at the same time or chat to your friends on Facebook! It seems that we really are reluctant to be present with our body as we once more disappear into the recesses of the chattering mind to multi- task to the greatest degree. Interestingly, research shows that multi-tasking actually decreases our ability to concentrate, leaving high multi-taskers less capable of identifying and filtering out irrelevant data. In complete contrast to this, mindful awareness or attention has been shown to produce and generate numerous health and wellness benefits. Recent studies have shown the almost endless list of health benefits from spending even just 15-20 minutes per day in traditional seated meditation. These health benefits include enhancing the immune system, reducing stress and anxiety levels, boosting memory and alertness and promoting happiness, inner peace and fulfilment in life. Pain levels are decreased whilst creativity and a sense of aliveness are heightened. However what is truly exciting is that Science also reveals that when meditation is taken a step further in the physical biological body through motion, it can not only offer these potent benefits, but can also really catalyse healing and health in the physical body itself.

This has powerful and far reaching implications in the fitness and health field. When you bring mindful attention to any part of the body that you are moving, you increase awareness and a direct somatic (body sense/feeling) experiencing of your body. This deepens and expands your own body spatial awareness. You become more able to sense the right way to move for *your* body. You start to be able to "listen" to the subtle messages and signals that your body may be sending you. You stop pushing harder or faster and seek to move differently or in a new way. You are able to identify which muscles are working too hard and can consciously relax other parts of your body that may be tensing up. Reading your email messages whilst you are exercising can never give you this. In fact they probably only serve to create more stress and tension, which is the last thing most of us desire to achieve.

The promise of romancing your body with movement invites you to come fully into the present moment whilst being open for the next movement and moment to reshape your destiny. The movements that I teach in my Chakranetics™ energy medicine fitness system are all designed to help you embody *more* of what you truly desire to *feel and experience* in your life. What we practice in the class becomes the destiny of our dreams in the "outside" world. When you weave meaning into movement and understand the meaning behind the moves you make, something extraordinary happens. You are set free to fully participate in your best, most vibrant and fulfilling life. Your consciousness is heightened as you fully embody your authentic destiny. You are no longer simply dreaming about what you want – you *are* what you want! There is a saying that goes, "You don't attract what you want, you attract who you are." I totally agree with this. You may want to be financially rich but unless you embody richness in every part of your being, money will always continue to be an issue. You can want to have a meaningful and loving relationship. However, unless you love yourself and create meaning in your life, this will always evade you. We cannot have what we do not embody.

Seven beautiful ways to romance your body with movement. Try these seven deliciously simple and loving movements to show your body how much you love it.

1. **The Abundance Smoothie - Awaken your body with abundance.** There is a beautiful and simple energy medicine movement that I do every morning before I get out of bed. It gently awakens my body as I begin a new day and puts me in the best possible state to receive abundance, joy, health, inner peace and positive energy. It's very easy to do. Sit on the edge of your bed with your spine long and feet flat upon the floor. Imagine that your feet have beautiful long, strong roots attached to them and they are connected right into the centre of the earth. See them immersed in the earth's rich soil. Imagine too that you have grown a fabulous long tail from the base of your spine that roots down into the earth's core. Feel your feet and your spine drinking in the richness and nourishment of the earth and flow this up your legs into the rest of your body. Feel connected, safe, centred, earthed and grounded. Take a few moments to connect inwards with your body. How do you feel? Are you tired or a bit achy? Or, are you feeling energised and ready to move into your day. Notice your energy levels without trying to change or judge them. Now, bring your hands together just in front of your lower belly and imagine that they are holding a golden, soft, shimmering ball of light. It's so light and radiant that it spills its luminescent glow all around you. Take a breath in through your nose and move your hands up the centre of your body, guiding this

soft golden light up towards the top of your head or crown chakra area. Exhale through your mouth with a gentle sigh as you turn your palms up and reach high into the space above your head. Extend your arms to the farthest that they can reach up above your head. Imagine you are lifting the light up and out into the Universe. Take another breath in and this time open your arms wide and float them out and open at your sides, palms upwards. Hold your arms out in this outstretched position for a moment or two. Feel your heart open as you look up slightly and smile. Imagine that you are receiving all that you desire in your life. I call this the abundance pose. Exhale and lower your arms down to your sides, turning your palms over so that they face the ground. As you turn your hands over, imagine that you are anchoring in all you desire. Return both hands back into the original starting position of holding the golden light energy ball. Imagine you are gathering up more energy and repeat the entire movement again. I often use body mantras in my movement work, whereby I attach a word or series of words to the movement and intention of the movement. You may like to use my mantras for this mindful movement exercise or you can make up your own. Mine are as follows: As you breathe in and raise your hands up your body say the words, "I breathe in." As your arms reach above your head, say the word, "Unlimited." As you open out your arms into the abundance pose, say the word "Abundance." And finally, as you return the arms back down to the start, say the words, "Now." You can say the words out loud or quietly in your head. Whatever suits you best. Repeat the entire sequence several times. You'll know when to stop because you will feel that it is enough. I generally find that just three rounds of this movement is enough to centre me and put me in a great place for the rest of my day, but do as many as you need. This movement can be done at any time of the day, but is especially good first thing in the morning as it helps to centre and ground you at the same time as opening your body, mind and heart to receiving more abundance, joy and love in your life.

2. **The beloved belly - Love your belly.** Our belly is often the area that has received such a tough time in our lives. In traditional fitness, dance or exercise programmes we have been instructed to hold the belly in, causing stress, tension and tightness in this area. Our relationship with our belly is often fraught with unkindness and disappointment in how it looks or feels. I used to hate my belly with a vengeance. I just didn't want it to be a part of me and spent far too many hours (years) of my life trying to flatten it, shrink it, reduce it and hide it! And, even when I had managed to shrink it to a certain degree, I *still* didn't like the way it looked. I mocked my belly endlessly calling it my "jelly belly." I undermined my poor belly with every word and thought I had, causing stress and tension in this area. I used to constantly suffer from stomach upsets – no wonder my stomach was upset. I would be upset if someone had treated me the way I treated my belly. Coming to love my belly has been a long process. Part of this process was looking at my belly in a completely new way. A way that was kind, loving, compassionate and deeply grateful. When you only view your belly according to its shape or size, you miss the pure beauty and essence that this area of your body carries. In energy medicine the belly is located in the second chakra energy field. In Sanskrit it means

the "Sacred home of the self." This area is our powerful deep emotional centre. It is here that pure creativity arises and is given birth by our feelings, dreams, fantasies and emotions. The belly longs to be loved. It craves your tenderness and wholehearted nourishment. More than anything the belly loves to be touched kindly – to feel your gentle hand caress your skin and feel your own softness within. It longs for you to embrace your own sweet curves and cradle them in your hands. Within your belly is your primal life force, the area you create from. It carries your dreams and stores your emotions. The belly is the storehouse of all of your most deep seated feelings and your greatest passions and sensuality. It is your finest protector and the giver and grower of days. It is the seat of contemplation and the place where the truest laughter and joy arises from in endless waves of belly laughs. When you hold your belly in your hands you hold your power, divine femininity and true creative source. Try this simple mindful movement meditation to come home to the core of your being – your beautiful belly. Sit quietly. Place your hands underneath your belly area as if you are cradling a baby. Breathe in through your nose, drawing your breath down into your lower belly. Allow your lower belly to expand slightly, feeling this gentle movement against your hands. As you exhale, allow your lower belly to relax back, softly and quietly. As you connect and cradle your belly, allow yourself to tap in to the vast wisdom and body of knowledge that your precious belly stores. Then, in a gentle loving motion begin to move your hands in a circular fashion over your belly. Begin at the bottom right of your belly and draw a circle up and around your entire abdominal area. Continue this gentle and loving massage. If any thoughts or critical judgements come up just notice them but don't attach to them. They are simply mind habits from your past. They are not the truth about who you really are. Focus back into your breath and continue to stay with the touch and the intention to connect with your belly. The belly's message is simple. If your belly could talk it might say, "*Listen to me. I speak in subtle ways – a shiver here, a tug, a pull, a gut feeling, a twinge, a flutter of excitement, a quake of fear, a heaviness, a lightness, a tingle and bubbles are all a part of my language. I am always talking with you. I am always reading your inner and outer world. I am the quickest way to know what is true. I can by-pass the mind – I'm quicker and more direct. I am instant. I am your deepest belief and I am your most ancient knowing. I am pure love. It is me that people look to for advice, for that inner spark of wisdom and insight – that gut feeling. Stretch marks cannot hide my beauty but many believe that I am ugly because of them. Scars cannot darken my landscape; they are simply physical maps of knowing, change, and healing. I am your life centre. Do you remember how sweet it was in the womb when you felt your mother's nourishment through the cord that bound us together. How blissful it was to know through the very centre of our being what it was like to be fed, nourished, to feel safe, attached and to belong. I long to feel that connection again with you. I long for you to embrace me, cradle me, and come home to me once more. To limit me simply to a shape or size is to limit your experience of life itself. Get to know me and love me. I will never steer you wrong. In my belly I trust. Let this be your mantra.*"

3. **The Belly Weave** - Another beautiful mindful movement for the belly is to weave figure eights with your hips. Stand with

your feet hip distance apart and allow your knees to soften slightly. Imagine that in front of you is a figure eight lying on its side. Gently begin to move your hips as if you are trying to draw the figure eight with them. Keep the movement small at first as your hips begin to map out its shape and gradually make the movement larger and more free flowing. Close your eyes and feel the sensuality and freedom this movement embodies. As with any movement or exercise, if you feel any discomfort, please stop and listen to your body.

1. **Dancing on shifting sands - Love your thighs.** This is a beautiful energy movement that really helps you to connect with where you are in the moment. The body always desires to know where it is. When you are full or worry or anxiety it can feel as if you aren't actually present in your body any more. You become caught up in the frenetic energy of the mind which is usually projecting some sort of anxious "story" about what might happen in the future. This can leave you feeling scattered or out of kilter. One of the best ways to move out of this fear based anxiety is to come back into the body. The "Dancing on shifting sands" exercise will help stabilise and support you and bring your energy right back down into your thighs, legs and feet. Begin by standing with your feet just wider than hip distance apart. Focus on your right foot and move your weight a fraction onto the left leg. As you do this imagine that you are drawing the right foot through the sand, really trying to stroke the floor with the sole of the foot as you lift and curl the right leg backwards into a hamstring curl. Place the right foot back down and repeat several times, each time really feeling as if you are trying to scoop up the floor with the underneath of your foot. Allow your hands to guide the energy

forward and back as you flow through this movement. Breathe in on the lift of the leg and out as you place the foot back down. Repeat the entire movement on the other side. This is a powerful exercise. The legs represent our personal strength and our trust in our own ability to move forward in life, take risks and change direction. Our feet are associated with security and survival. They are about completing tasks or projects and reaching our goals. As you perform the shifting sands movement be aware of learning to keep readjusting according to what life is offering you. To learn to dance on shifting sands is to be able to stay grounded, secure, balanced and strong even in the most difficult of challenges.

2. **Angel Kisses – Love your face.** We live behind our faces and look out at the world through the mirrors of our eyes. What we perceive the world to be is a reflection of who we are, what we believe, think and feel to be true. Unless we spend all day in front of a mirror we rarely get to see the beauty and subtle changes of how our face changes throughout the day. So often we are unaware of just how beautiful we look when we are happy or engaged in a project we love. We don't see our own eyes when they are full of tenderness or love. We never experience the sweet relaxed look on our faces when we are deeply asleep and the world's worries have fallen from our brows. Much of the time we tend to have a fixed image or perception of how we may look or appear to others. This often is rooted in the past or in some kind of negative old "conditioning" about how we *should* look. The "Angel Kisses" exercise invites you to appreciate and love your face. Sit comfortably and close your eyes. Allow your focus to turn inwards and become

aware of your breathing. Rub both hands together vigorously and then very gently, tap your fingers very lightly all over your face. Allow a soft smile to light up your lips as you bestow on your skin hundreds of these tiny "Angel Kisses." It's a beautiful way to boost your complexion and show love to your own face. Finish off the exercise by placing your hands on either sides of your cheeks and just cup your face in your hands. This is such an easy and loving movement to do for the people we love and care about, however we seldom take time to do it for ourselves.

3. **Reboot Vitality – Love your pelvis.** This simple and powerfully re-energising movement nourishes and nurtures your pelvic area, base of your spine, hips and pelvic floor. In energy medicine this is the area of the root chakra, which sends its life affirming energy down through your legs and up your spine. Sit on a chair or on the edge of your bed with your feet flat on the floor. Very slowly and gently roll your spine backwards and downwards, allowing the hips to tuck under. Feel your body contracting and shortening as you round out your spine. When you have rolled back and down as far as you can comfortably go, begin to roll upwards and forwards. Lengthen and straighten your spine whilst allowing your pelvis to roll forward and your bottom to stick out slightly – pushing behind you on the chair or bed. You will also feel your heart area expanding and broadening as you begin to lengthen your spine. Allow your shoulders to ease back, as if your shoulder blades are trying to kiss each other. Let your belly be soft and relaxed as you roll your pelvis gently forward. Breathe in as you rock forward and exhale as you flow backwards in this soft subtle pelvic tilting and rocking movement. Imagine

there is a beautiful vivid red rose at the base of your spine and with each rock forward and backwards it opens and uncurls its petals a little more. This energy movement brings vitality, safety, groundedness and stability in your life. It reignites passion and creativity and confidence. This area of our body often becomes stuck and stiff, especially if you are experiencing anxiety or fear. Other physical problems associated with an imbalanced root chakra area are issues with the lower back, colon and bladder. Leg or problems with the feet may also occur. Eating disorders are also associated with an imbalance in this area. When this area is balanced, fluid and flowing you feel supported, safe and completely connected to your deepest guidance.

4. **The tricep prayer – Love your arms.** The tricep prayer is a beautiful, strong and deeply connective exercise. Our arms carry and embrace what we love in our lives. They hold and hug or push away and protect. When we believe we are going to be hurt in some way our arms come up to protect our faces or the body part which we are trying to keep safe. The arms are an extension of the heart in energy medicine work, as is the upper back and rib cage. When you open your heart, you also open your arms. When you close your heart, your arms also close inwards causing the shoulders to round forward and the spine to round outwards. As with so much of our body, the arms are often judged for how they look rather than how they feel. Try this loving mindful movement exercise to reconnect your heart, your desires and what you want to embrace more of in your life. Begin by sitting or standing, whichever feels more comfortable for you. Place your hands together in prayer position just in

front of your heart area. Rub your hands together as you charge the Chi energy between your palms. Breathe in and move your hands away from each other. Imagine you are drawing the energy outwards to the sides of your body like strands of golden honey. Breathe out and turn the hands away from each other as if you are trying to stretch and push out into the furthest reaches of space. Breathe in and turn your palms upwards, raising both arms above your head. Imagine you are gathering golden light upwards above your head. Bring both hands together in prayer position and softly allow your hands to lower behind your head. You may be aware of your entire chest and heart area expanding and opening as you do this movement. Only drop your hands back as far as you can comfortably go. Imagine pointing the fingers down your spine and directing loving flow and energy right through and down your your spinal column. Remember this is not about how far you can go or how well you can perform an exercise. This is about connecting to the deep wisdom of your body and allowing yourself to fully embody all that you desire in your life. Essentially it's all about love, kindness, curiosity and compassion. When you have these four elements in place in all that you do, life expands to welcome more of the authentic YOU. Your body naturally moves into a place of health, harmony and healing. Rest for a moment with the hands at the back of your head in prayer position and then gently raise your arms up above the head once more, breathe in as you extend your arms up to the Universe (hands still in prayer pose). Breathe out as you lower both arms down in front of your body to come back in alignment with the heart chakra area. Repeat the movement from the beginning but miss out rubbing your palms together. Close your eyes and experience this movement from the inside out. Never be tempted to judge how you are doing the move, just allow your self to flow with your breath, your awareness, your intention and your experience of what is actually happening in the moment.

5. **Hand whispers – Love your creativity.** If the body is the physical container of your story, then your hands are the directors and communicators of your intentions, desires and purpose. The hands are like verbs. They say how something is to be done. They carry intention, creativity, intensity, passion, meaning and energetic flow. They can be used to accentuate or modify a movement according to what you desire. If you watch people as they talk, their hands will often direct or embellish the story they are telling. Indeed some people find it really difficult to speak if they are not allowed to use their hands to communicate. In mindful movement and energy medicine work the hands provide the emotional and directional content of the movement. There is great energy and healing in our hands. We automatically place our hands on someone when they are upset or in distress. When we feel upset, our hands automatically come up and touch our own heart, seeking to calm and reassure the emotion we are feeling. We shake hands when we meet new people. We use our hands to generate trust and support in light touches of praise for another – a pat on the back. Our hands can hold onto things with force and tension or we can let go and open our hands in surrender and trust that everything is happening exactly as it needs to. Consciously using your hands in mindful movement opens you into a completely new

dimension of awareness. Try this hand whisper meditation to focus your mind and connect with your innermost being. Sit comfortably with your hands facing palm upwards in your lap. Breathe in through the back of your hands and out through your open palms. What would you most love to create in your life right now? What would give you more joy, health, love or freedom? As you consciously continue to breathe in through the backs of your hands and out through the front, allow your mind to set an intention for this meditation. Notice how your hands are in an open position of receiving as they rest gently on your lap. Take your right hand and place the index and middle finger in the centre of your left palm. Feel the touch of your fingers on your skin. Begin to gently tap the centre of the palm with your fingers. Say out loud or in your head, "I am here." Moving your fingers in an anticlockwise circle on the palm repeat quietly to yourself, "I now release.... (say whatever you want to let go of or release from your life). What has been stopping you from achieving what you truly wish for? Keep the anti clockwise circle going until you have named all of the things that you feel have kept you stuck or have got in the way. Close your left palm over your fingers and hold gently and firmly. When you feel ready, open your left hand and brush the fingers of your right hand along the palm as if you are brushing off tiny grains of dust or sand. Continue until you feel that all of the dust has gone. Imagine it falling back to the earth where it becomes a rich fertile compost for new growth and new beginnings. Turn your right palm over and with your left hand place the index and middle finger into the centre of your palm. Tap the palm gently as you say, "I am here." Moving your fingers in a clockwise circle, repeat quietly to yourself, "I now receive...(say whatever it is you wish to allow more of into your life. When you feel ready, gently close the fingers of your right hand around the index and middle finger of your left hand and hold lovingly and firmly. Open out your right hand and bring both hands together in a soft prayer position without the palms touching each other. (There should be a space in the middle of both hands). The heels of your hands and your fingers are touching. Keeping the heels of your hands together open out your hands as if you are opening up a story book. Say to yourself, "And so begins a new story." Anchor the movement by bringing the right hand to your heart area and the left hand to your lower belly. Breathe deeply and fully as you allow this new chapter and story become fully embodied in your life.

Make movement your medicine

Movement has always been something that I have returned to again and again. It didn't really matter what kind of movement it was – I just felt more alive and more connected to me, the world and life when I moved. When we move we are in the flow of our life. There is a sense and purpose to our days. Life floods through our body and calls us again and again to keep growing, expanding, changing, learning and transforming. Movement has been shown to help with depression, anxiety, stress and low confidence. Even changing the posture of your body has the ability to transform the way you are feeling. When the body moves in a new way, the brain also has to move in alignment with this. Equally, when you choose a new way of thinking, this information infuses the body with a different chemical response and therefore a new movement pattern in response. The body and mind are inextricably linked – when one changes the other also adapts and follows suit and vice versa. This is exciting because it means that we have huge amounts of power in determining our own state of health if we make certain movement choices. Indeed, research has shown that moderate cardiovascular movement exercise for 30 - 45 minutes, 3 - 4 times a week has literally grown brain volume within the frontal cortex and hippocampus, an area associated with spatial memory and part of the limbic system (emotional brain) by as much as 2% and this was in participants aged 60-80 years old!

For me, more than anything else, movement helps me to connect with all of who I am. We live in exciting and challenging times. There is so much in our daily environment that distracts and takes our focus away from whom we authentically are. We can see the signs of this disconnection and separation from mind, body, heart and spirit all around us. When I return to the rise and fall of my breath, when I stretch and dance or go out walking I am guided "home" again to the truth of my authenticity and who I really am. Allow yourself to be moved by your life. When in doubt or feeling stuck – just move, take action! It doesn't really matter what movement you do – just MOVE! Get into the flow again. Get up and walk, run on the spot, dance, wiggle, stretch, bend forward, bend backwards, walk sideways, skip, raise your knees, point your toes, breathe in deeply and exhale fully. Just move! Everything else will take care of itself as your body begins to flow with energy again. The best lotion is the body in motion – it mobilises the joints, activates the lymph, improves blood circulation, wakes up the mind, calms the nervous system, releases stress and promotes that fabulous feel good factor! So, romance your body with movement!

8

ROMANCE YOUR BODY WITH COMPASSION

My Darling You

Think of me as the most beautiful present you have ever received...

Unwrap me tenderly
Marvel at how wonderful I am
Dress me up and show me off
And most of all, share your gift with the world!
Always present for you!
Body xx

I ALWAYS PRIDED myself on being so open hearted and loving. If anyone was hurt or feeling down, I would be there in an instant. I thought nothing of spending as much time as they needed to comfort, listen or reassure them that everything would be okay. Compassion and empathy flowed from me like an endless stream, soothing the hurts and fears of others. And yet, when it came to being compassionate to myself, I failed miserably. I just couldn't seem to do it. I simply had no tolerance for my own hurts, fears, woes or sadness. If I felt down, I told myself to "get on with it!" If I was afraid or nervous about an event or situation, I barely gave myself the time of day to heed those worries. I just pushed myself through it. When I stubbed my toe the first thoughts weren't compassionate or caring they were harsh and unfeeling. I blamed myself for being clumsy – I should have looked where I was going. And yet if that had been a friend of mine I would have said that I was sorry she had hurt herself. I would have acknowledged her pain and asked her if she was okay. Isn't it interesting how we avoid being loving caring and compassionate with ourselves and yet find it so easy to shower others with our tenderness, love and kindness? It's all part of the way that we don't show ourselves the kind of respect and cherishing we deserve. Why? Because, for the most part we haven't learned *how* to. As I have spoken about previously, how we were tended to when we were hurt in childhood has a great influence in how we will tend to ourselves in adulthood. It's worth mentioning again as so often we blame ourselves for our sense of lack or shortcomings. We forget that 95% of our behaviour was learned and is still playing out its old recording today in the way we treat ourselves. As children our pain may have been minimised by parents who told us that "It was nothing" or not to be silly because it's only a scratch. Our parents may have been too busy to sit down with us and hold us gently until the pain had gone. Perhaps they felt inadequate to help us deal with our hurt or felt too upset when we were upset to be fully present for us. There are many reasons and none of them are about blaming our parents or primary caretakers – just understanding where our first lessons in compassion came from and what we learned. Equally, as children we learn how our parents take care of their own pain and suffering. We model our behaviour on the behaviour we witness in our family. The mother who always blames herself when things go wrong, the father who stoically denies he has any pain and keeps on pushing through despite the agony on his face. We watch and we learn how our family manage the things that upset or hurt them. When I think back to my own mother's way of coping with her grief after my father had died, she shut herself away. She poured herself a few glasses of sherry, disappeared into a few packets of crisps and smiled broadly through uncried tears. When I asked her what was wrong she would shake her head rather too brightly and say "Nothing!" If I asked her if she had been crying she would tell me she had something in her eye or it was just a cold that was coming on. She seemed to suffer from an endless stream of colds and things in her eye! I know that she was probably trying to protect me from seeing her sadness but I could feel it anyway and simply felt confused by what I intuitively felt and what she said. And so I, too, learned how to use food as a coping mechanism and to smile even though I was crying inside.

If Pain is the question – Compassion is the answer.

When we are in pain the last thing we want to do is to actually *BE* with that pain. We try to get away from it, to shut it up or numb it out. We want it to go away and very often would do anything to make that happen. Pain is a demanding teacher. It insists on your attention all of the time – why? Because it's doing it's job. It's telling you that something needs to be addressed. It's asking for your help, your focus, your love and your understanding. Ultimately, pain is always a request for change and invites you to address the situation. When I first developed Arthritis, the last thing I felt was love for my body. I was in acute pain, which turned into chronic pain. I resented the pain and the lack of mobility in my joints. I had been trained as a dancer in my early life and felt so much anger towards my body for not being able to do the things that I once loved. I was angry at my body and I demanded that it go back to how it once was. However, my body in it's own inimitable way had other ideas and I began a journey of learning to really love and "talk" to my body in ways that I once would have thought impossible.

The major shift came when I realised that although I had physical pain, I was causing myself tremendous *suffering* by my attitude towards my body and the pain. The more I focused on what I *couldn't* do, the more I suffered. The more I looked at the body I had and lamented over the body I had "lost," the more pain I felt. Every time I tried to get away from my pain instead of being present in the moment, I created more resistance and struggle within every part of me.

One of the most loving and healing ways to help manage pain is to get in touch with the emotional side of pain. Pain brings up so many emotions that need to be acknowledged, released and healed. When we are able to connect with the emotional feelings that pain brings up, we are able to stop causing suffering within ourselves. The physical pain may still be present, however we are able to soften around it and not suffer because of it. This can make a huge difference to how we manage pain and the intensity of the feelings. Ultimately it is about changing the way that we perceive pain and developing a relationship with it that can be managed and healed. It can also help speed up recovery.

We are extraordinary intelligent heart sentient beings who have the ability to "read" the field of energy from other people, environments and our own emotional state of being. However, most of us were not trained or taught to use this naturally occurring skill in a positive manner. In fact for many of us, we were taught how *not* to love ourselves or take time to really appreciate and care for our own happiness, health and well being. We have been taught to disregard our body's signals and messages for rest and tenderness as we continue to keep going far longer than we really should. The pain medication adverts on television reinforce this message constantly as they encourage us to pop a pill so that we can go on with what we had planned as if nothing was wrong. The body is silenced and dumbed down again and again as its intuitive voice is viewed as an inconvenience rather than a warning signal that something may be wrong and needs help and loving attention. These days we haven't got time to be ill and yet more and more people are suffering with fatigue, digestive disorders, inflammation, auto immune disorders, allergies, depression and chronic pain.

Staggeringly "Almost half the adult population is living with chronic pain," The Daily Mail reports. A major new review suggests that some type of chronic pain affects around 28 million adults in the UK. In the USA people living with chronic pain are more than 100 million Americans. As someone who has experienced living with chronic pain for over fifteen years I know only too well the debilitating effects that this can have on your life and more importantly the relationship you have with you! When you are unable to get away from the pain you feel in your body, (physical, mental and emotional), there is nowhere to go and you become a prisoner within your own skin. This in turn produces more feelings of upset and distress, which heightens your pain response and locks your body into more and more inflammation and rigidity. Pain changes the relationship you have with yourself unless you are able to change the relationship you have with pain. I would like to share with you one technique that I have used in my own pain management and also with the many clients that I work with.

The Compassionate Conversation Meditation.

The following technique is a process or a conversation in the form of a guided meditation that I invite you to have with the pain. It works well when someone can guide you through it personally, however, you could also do it alone. My suggestion is that you record the words and guidelines and play it back to yourself. I also have recordings of this technique available on my website at www.astridlonghurst.com

Begin by making yourself as comfortable as possible. Either sitting or lying down. Make sure that you won't be disturbed for a while and make sure that you are as warm and relaxed as possible.

Close your eyes and begin to turn your attention to your breathing.
Just notice the rise and fall of your chest and the gentle way the air enters and leaves your body.
There is no need to change the way you are breathing just become more aware of how you don't have to do anything in order to breathe.
It's so easy and it happens without you having to force it or will yourself to breathe.
Just notice how easy it is to breathe and how your body does this all on its own.
Imagine that you are drawing the breath all the way down into your lower belly.
Feel your lower belly expand outwards just a fraction as you breathe in.
Then allow your lower belly to relax and deflate a little as you breathe out.
Feel as if you are inviting the breath all the way through to your lower belly area. Imagine it filling your entire pelvic area and softening into the back of your body. Imagine your lower spine drinking in the soft warm air as you breathe in.
Imagine the breath flowing up your spine and out of your body as you exhale.
Every breath is a kind breath – a loving breath – a gentle breath.
Allow your breath to flow into every part of your body, relaxing and calming you.
Now, allow yourself to notice where your physical pain is in your body. Just notice the area without judgment, opinion or criticism. What is the emotional *feeling* that this pain brings up for you? Be

aware of how you are feeling. What is the emotion? For example, you may feel anger, sadness, frustration, fear, vulnerability, insecurity, impatience, boredom, resentment. Just see if you can get in touch with the emotional feeling of your pain. You may feel more than one emotion. Just go with the strongest emotion that you are aware of.

Where do you feel this emotion? Is it only in the area of physical pain or is it else where in your body?

If you can, place your hand over the area of this emotion and connect with the feeling. Just be present for the feeling.

I'm going to ask you some questions about this emotion or feeling. Just be aware of anything that comes into your mind or awareness in response to the questions. Bear in mind that you may not get an answer right away, that's okay. It may come later for you. The important thing is simply to connect with the feeling and ask the questions.

Question1: If this feeling had a shape, what shape would it be?

Question 2: If this shape had a colour, what colour would it be?

Question 3: Does this shape move?

Question 4: If this shape moves, how does it move? Where does it want to go?

Question 5: If this shape had a sound, what sound would it make?

Question 6: If this shape had a texture, what texture would it be?

Question 7: If this shape could speak, what would it say?

Notice what's there. It's like an aspect of you that has been stuck in a moment of trauma or pain and has been calling to you to notice it. The only way it could get your attention was through physical pain. But now, you have noticed it and it's up to you to let this emotion, this feeling know that you are present.

Imagine that you have become the observer of this part of

you. Imagine that you are witnessing this feeling, this shape, with love, empathy and kindness.

Begin to talk to this part of you by saying the following words out loud. Imagine you are saying these words to this part of you that has been feeling so much pain. Repeat out loud after me:

I'm so sorry that you hurt
I'm so sorry that you've been in so much pain
I'm so sorry that you have hurt for so long
I'm here now
I'm present
I'm not going anywhere
I've got you
I see you
I care about how you feel
And you don't have to change
You don't have to go anywhere
You're safe now
I'm here for you
I'm present
It's okay to feel what you feel
I've got you
Thank you for letting me know how you feel
Thank you for being here
Thank you for enduring this pain
You are welcome here – you don't have to go anywhere
I'm here. I've got you and you're safe now.

Take a deep full breath in and exhale gently on a sigh. Repeat this a few times. Feel what you feel, be fully in this moment.

Now gently ask this emotion – this feeling – this shape what it needs. You may want to ask it a few times. What does it need? What can you do for this feeling?

Be aware of any answer that comes up for you. Your answer

may come in words or a sense of knowing. You may get a feeling about what it needs or get an image of something. There is no right or wrong way to do this – just go with whatever you are experiencing, even if you are not aware of experiencing anything at all.

Place one hand over your heart area and quietly say out loud in an "I am statement" of what this emotion needs. Identify what the feeling is. For example, if you got the sense of needing the pressure to be released or more support, you would say "I AM FREE, I AM SUPPORTED"

If you were aware of this part of you as needing love, you would say, "I AM LOVED"

If this part of you needed to be seen or heard, you would say, "I AM SEEN, I AM HEARD!"

If you were aware of needing to be accepted, valued, shown kindness to, you would say.

"I AM ACCEPTED"

"I AM VALUED"

"I AM KIND"

If you get a visual image as an answer then just say what the image is, for example, if you saw an image of the ocean then simply say "I AM THE OCEAN!"

Repeat this "I AM" statement a few times with your eyes closed and your hand over your heart area.

When you feel ready, just open your eyes slowly, bringing your awareness back into the room or environment around you. Notice your breathing, stretch your body a little, move your fingers and toes and come back fully into the moment.

Understanding the process

You may want to write down any insight you had during this process. Sometimes things that you may have experienced during this meditation don't seem to make any sense. Write it down anyway and allow yourself to process what you experienced. You may get an answer later in the day or even in the following weeks or months.

The body mind speaks in very literal and metaphoric ways. One of my clients had an image of her painful emotion as being a table. This table was wooden and sturdy and didn't move. It couldn't move because it had masses of books and stuff piled on top of it. When I asked her the question, "If this shape could speak, what would it say?" she recalled that it said "I can't bear it anymore!"

She realised that she had been carrying every body else's stuff for years! She took on other people's problems and became completely involved in other people's lives to the point that her own life and self care was completely neglected. She literally couldn't *bear* it anymore! Interestingly her physical pain was located in her lower spine and down one leg. Her own support system was collapsing under the weight of trying to hold everyone else up.

This was a huge insight for her.

When we got to the part of the body dialogue that asked the question, "What do you need?" Her answer was instant. She needed to be free and to feel supported. She began using the "I AM statement of "I AM FREE AND I AM SUPPORTED!"

This helped her deal with her chronic pain in several ways. The first was that she began to take on less things that others wanted her to do. She began to say "No" more often to the things that weighed her down or she found a burden and began to say "Yes" to the things and people that gave her more joy.

She used the mantra/affirmation of "I am free and I am supported" throughout her days.

The image of the table was such a powerful one for her and she decided to change the table from the sturdy wooden table into a light, pretty glass table that only had a single vase and flower on it!

You have to feel to heal!

You may find that you experience an outpouring of emotion from doing the above exercise. Please just allow yourself to express what you feel – don't hold back. This is all part of the healing process. So often we have trapped our emotional voice in physical pain – sometimes for years! This exercise helps you to reconnect and get in touch with these emotions and helps you release and express them in a safe and gentle way. The beauty of this body dialogue is that it helps you to get in touch with the pain in a completely different way. The last thing that many people want to do when they are in pain is to be anywhere near it. This creates more stress, struggle and resistance, which can heighten pain levels. When you can accept what is happening, you can deal with the situation better. When you allow the pain to be your guide you are able to understand the way that it changes, moves, ebbs and flows. The Compassionate Conversation meditation provides a space in which you can begin to talk to the pain and the emotions that surround it.

For me (and my clients), this makes a huge difference because I realise that I am *not* my pain. I am so much *more* than my pain and the emotions I am feeling. I can separate my identity from my pain and in that moment I am able to manage my pain better. This is powerful because pain can be all consuming to the point that you feel that *all* of you is in pain. This technique helps you to be there for your pain and gives the emotions a chance to be felt and expressed. The mind-body connection is extraordinarily powerful and just the simple act of beginning a conversation with your pain and getting in touch with your emotions can help promote healing and better self management. This has a powerful effect on the parasympathetic nervous system as you allow yourself to move into a relaxed and calmer way of being, rather than staying in the high stress response of the sympathetic nervous system (fight, flight or freeze).

You may also find that as you continue to do the Compassionate Conversation meditation, the image of your pain changes. Another good exercise is also to begin to visualise an image that would be more helpful and positive – just as my client did in changing the sturdy table image into a small glass table. As you continue to be in communication with your emotions you also free up energy in your body. Remember that all an emotion ever wants is to be felt and expressed.

Romancing your body with compassion means that you begin to learn to hold your own body with a gentle care and kindness and sensitivity to what you are feeling or experiencing. Compassion connects and brings us back to the *wholeness* of who we are and also our deepest sense of belonging. It is the key element in all emotional healing and spiritual awakening. When we are divided against ourself in any way we become fragmented, disconnected and out of touch with the beauty and powerful presence of the being we truly are. The heart of compassion begins with yourself. When you turn towards your own pain or suffering with awareness and an intention to be kind, you end the body wars and open up a completely new way of *being* with you. These days, I am kinder to myself. When I stub my toe, I stop and allow the pain to be felt and released through my body. I tell my toe I'm sorry that it hurts. I pause and spend a while acknowledging the painful experience until I feel ready to move on. I would have never done this in the past. Just the idea of telling my toe I was sorry would have seemed ridiculous. I would have simply sworn loudly, told myself off and tried to carry on with what I was doing despite this inconvenience.

How do you relate to your suffering?

When you feel stuck or are in pain, do you ignore it or immediately go into problem solving mode? Maybe you judge yourself for not being able to sort it out. Do you mentally beat yourself up or give yourself a hard time? Perhaps you use whatever has happened to you to prove to yourself that you really aren't good enough? Or maybe you dismiss and minimise your pain by saying that others have it worse? What would happen if you paused and acknowledged the pain that you felt? What if you took a moment to feel what you are feeling and then extend kindness and compassion to yourself? What if you made it your primary intention to be kinder towards you? What if you made a choice that it was simply unacceptable to hurt yourself anymore? When met with the choice to turn away from your pain or discomfort, imagine if you chose to be with that pain, no matter what. We cause untold suffering when we turn on ourselves or make who we are and what we feel wrong in any way. You are not wrong. You're not broken and there's nothing to fix. There is only love, kindness, empathy, warmth and compassion. This is our natural state of being. We automatically reach out to our loved ones when they are in pain, however, we seldom do this in the same way to ourselves. To hold yourself in your own tender loving care is one of the most beautiful things you can do for you. When a child is hurt they need acknowledgment that they are in pain. They seek to be swept up in love, care and the knowledge that someone is there who can help ease their hurt. What would happen if YOU were always there for YOU? Imagine that you decided not to ignore what you were feeling or try to figure it out or blame yourself in any way for what hurts. Imagine that you pressed pause on life and stopped to be with what was hurting you in the moment. Imagine that you talked to yourself in tender tones of love. Imagine that you said to yourself, "It's okay, I'm here, I've got you. I'm right here and I'm not going anywhere." At the very least you might feel a little more comforted. At the very best you may find that your hurt and pain becomes an integrated and valued part of your life experience and eventually disappears. There is beauty and magic when you can take care of your pain and allow it to be there because it is a part of you. When you meet your pain with compassion you are free to change. A recent quote from The New York Times says, "The research suggests that giving ourselves a break and accepting our imperfections may be the first step towards better health. People who score high on tests of self-compassion have less depression and anxiety and tend to be happier and more optimistic."

Mindful Caring is the key to Compassion

One key element of compassion is mindfulness. When you become aware that you are hurting in some way or just feel off kilter, you can bring mindful caring to the part of you that hurts. This means that you slow down and tune into the feelings you are experiencing without judgment or being critical. So often we feel that if we can just control ourselves we will be better. However, this often leads to a glossing over or a "masking" of what is trying to be born and heard within us. When we push down, suppress or try to stop what we are feeling we move into the trance of separateness. We feel alone, disconnected, numb, not okay and as if no one else cares about us. This is just an illusion but it feels so real. When ever you push away, you resist yourself and the truth of the moment. The truth of the moment may be that you hurt or feel pain but even in this suffering the truth is also that you are valid, loved, beautiful and powerful beyond measure. Imagine that a loved one was feeling down or hurting in some way. We would sit down with them and ask them what was wrong. We would listen and spend time trying to understand their fears or what was upsetting them. Romancing your body with compassion means that you extend this same loving care to yourself. It means bringing your awareness tenderly to the moment you are inhabiting and being mindful of what is present. Instead of making yourself wrong in any way, you can recognise that things are tough and offer yourself kindness instead. Compassion comes out of the awareness of suffering. It is the glue of connection to the Self. And in the place of awareness you have a choice. There is a small space that opens up that offers you a glimmer of hope. You can choose to continue to be tough on yourself and indulge in old reactive behaviour or, you can choose to be kind. The space where kindness sits is the place we find our own personal truth, love and freedom.

Cultivate self-compassion with the AAAAh technique

Self compassion, like any other skill has to be learned, especially if we were not taught how to love and look after ourselves as a first priority. Use this simple AAAAh technique to help you begin to practice romancing your body with compassion.

1. **A = Acknowledge** the suffering. Recognise that you are having a hard time. Tune into what is happening right now for you in the moment. What are you feeling? Are you angry? Afraid? Upset? Sad? Name the feeling and be mindful of not trying to fix it. Remind yourself that everyone feels this feeling at different points in their life. You are not alone.
2. **A = Allow** what's there to be there. Stop resisting the feeling and drop the struggle. This is part of being alive. These feelings are allowed to be present and the key is to be able to begin to get comfortable with the uncomfortable. Pause, breathe and say to yourself, "May I offer myself the compassion I need."
3. **A = Ask** what you are believing about the situation right now. Where and how is this feeling in your body? Investigate the thoughts around the feelings. How long have you felt this way? Ask, "Who would you be if you didn't believe that something was wrong with you?" Who would you be if you loved yourself unconditionally? Take your left hand hand and hold it

gently with your right hand. Feel your own presence and gentle touch. What is it like to hold yourself with kindness?

4. **A = Authenticity.** When you really care, you can be with your own suffering and contact what is going on inside of you. Then you can grow, blossom, melt and expand into the love of your own being. You are no longer avoiding, suppressing, distracting, judging or resisting what you feel. There is no need to pretend that everything is fine. There is no more demanding that things or life be anything other than what they are. There is a peace and deep acceptance that comes from owning ALL of you! No longer fragmented or feeling separate from ourselves we can reach out to ourself for love and find that we are there. We know that we will never leave or abandon ourself again. For me, this is the ultimate place of my own personal healing. When I no longer ran or hid from my hurts, insecurities or pain I began to open up a healing space in my heart where I could reside in peace.
5. **H = Healing.** Healing is just one of the natural side-effects of this process. What words of kindness can you offer yourself right now? What would you most love to hear? Imagine what you would love to hear a loved one say to you and then say it to yourself. Some suggestions are, You're beautiful, it's okay, I love you, I'm here, take your time, I'm with you, You're safe, you don't have to do anything right now, everything is exactly as it needs to be, you are loved.

I love this poem by Dana Faulds called Awakening Now

Why wait for your awakening?
The moment your eyes are open,

seize the day. Would you hold
back when the Beloved beckons?
Would you deliver your litany
of sins like a child's collection
of sea shells, prized and labeled?
"No, I can't step across the
threshold," you say, eyes
downcast. "I'm not worthy"
I'm afraid, and my motives
aren't pure. I'm not perfect,
and surely I haven't practiced
nearly enough. My meditation
isn't deep, and my prayers are
sometimes insincere. I still chew
my fingernails, and the refrigerator
isn't clean." Do you value your
reasons for staying small more
than the light shining through
the open door? Forgive yourself.
Now is the only time you have
to be whole. Now is the sole
moment that exists to live in
the light of your true Self.
Perfection is not a prerequisite
for anything but pain. Please,
oh please, don't continue to
believe in your disbelief, your stories
of separation and failure.

This is the day of your awakening.

9

ROMANCE YOUR BODY WITH UNCONDITIONAL LOVE

To the one I love
If you want to have the most passionate life you can ever have...
Fall in love with me!
I'll be waiting!
(It will be an affair to remember!)
Yours, passionately, Body x

There is something happening in the world right now that is heralding the dawn of a truly conscious change in the way that we view ourselves. More and more people are "waking up" to their own awesomeness, beauty and divinity. No longer prepared to accept what the mainstream media tells them about who they are and what they want, people all over the world are rising up and taking charge of their own lives, feelings, health and vitality. As we leave behind the old ways of thinking, living and believing we step into a new paradigm which calls us to truly LOVE ALL of who we are. As we allow the "old self" to leave, it is important that we let go of who we were with love and great gratitude. The "old self" is the one that got us through. It managed to take us to this point in time where we stand now on the brink of change. We couldn't have got here without all of our old behaviours, thoughts, fears and "stories." Loving who we *are* means loving who we *were* and realising that every step of our journey was exactly right and perfect just as it was. This can be a tough challenge for some people. It was for me. Why on earth would we choose to suffer and go through so much pain? Surely there had to be a better, easier way for us to grow and evolve past our most limiting beliefs and behaviours! I found myself wondering if I really had to hate my body so much and be so self-destructive throughout so many years of my life. I thought back to the ways that I never showed myself love. My out of control eating, my toxic, hurtful and negative thinking, my anger, my judgements and opinions and the way I simply cut people out of my life if they didn't do what I wanted them to do. I remembered the games I played and the people I hurt. I thought back to the money I spent on slimming pills, fad diets and painful treatments to shrink my fat. I recalled the arguments I had and the rage I felt with others because they just didn't seem to understand me. So many days where I took to my bed because I couldn't face the world or how I looked in the world. Memories of walking along the local high street at the age of twelve and being yelled at by the local gang of cool kids. "Look at her – she's pregnant! Or is it just FAT" the taunts were cruel and cut deeply into my young body. Anyone who has ever suffered because of the way that they look will know how distressing and painful it can be. And yet, somehow and rather miraculously my body got me through to face another day and then another day. My incredible body that took so many insults – not just from others but from me too. As I sit here writing these words, I know without a shadow of a doubt that everything I went through was vital for me to become the woman that I am today. I used to think that I had wasted so much of my life by the way that I had treated myself. There were so many opportunities that I just couldn't take because I didn't feel adequate or up for the job. There were so many days that I wasn't present because I couldn't be in the moment. I know now that none of these moments were wasted. They were all exactly as they needed to have been, because in those long dark nights of the body and soul I was incubating the Self that was getting ready to be born. The stages of growth are often unseen. The small and almost imperceptible shifts in the way the body and mind are formed often take place in the dark. The strongest of roots in any plant form long before you see the flower or the blossom. You might be forgiven for thinking that nothing significant is happening when you plant a seed and see nothing for weeks. And yet, deep in the fertile rich soil of the land, extraordinary changes are taking place as life grows itself. It is the same for us. The richness of our soil are the vast landscapes of our experiences, encounters, emotions and environments. And although we may not feel that it is rich or indeed fertile, we are in exactly the right place at the right time. The secret is to allow ourselves to bloom and flourish in these sometimes seemingly inhospitable conditions.

A client of mine spoke despairingly about her inability to love herself. She came to me at her lowest ebb and didn't know where else to go or what to do. As I listened she told me about the way she had treated her body. She cried over the addictions to drugs, food and sex. She winced in pain as she spoke about her boyfriend of five years who had done everything in his power to help her and yet she had cheated on him countless times. I asked her gently if she could have changed any of the things that she had told me about at the time they were happening. Could she have done anything differently? She answered, "No."

I continued with another question. I wondered if what she did was simply the best that she could do at the time? Given that she didn't know another way of being or coping, were her actions all that she could do?

She nodded her head.

"Yes," she said. I didn't know another way. I just did what I did to survive."

She continued, "I didn't like what I was doing – the drinking and the drugs, but they made me feel better. They took the edge off my feelings. They numbed me out so that I could have sex and pretend for a wild moment that I was loved, wanted and safe."

As we continued to work together she realised that everything she had done had been in order to protect and look after the fragile small self that felt unloved and unsafe in this world. We all do what we can with what we have. As Maya Angelou (poet and author) once said, *"When we know better, we do better."*

Romancing your body with love isn't just a nice idea or some kind of fanciful notion. It's essential for your greatest health and optimum well being. How you feel about yourself, your body and your life has the power to impact every part of your life, especially your health, vitality and overall well being. Unconditional love is the core quality of the heart. When you bring the *feeling* quality of love to every part of your life and your Self, you are positively changing and charging your inner and outer environment. The qualities of the heart have long been spoken about in literature, music, poetry, sports and every kind of relationship. We say words like, "Follow your heart, or listen to your heart." We encourage people to put more heart into something they are doing. When we are afraid or angry with ourself or someone else we close down our hearts or lose heart. When in love we experience the intoxicating feeling of being open hearted. We not only love the one we're with but we feel in love with the whole world also. As mentioned earlier on in this book, love is a verb – it is an active process of something we feel and desire to feel. Love is also a choice and something that we need to actively and consciously select in the way that we live and the way that we are with who we are. Although the heart is a physical organ pumping the blood around our body, it is also so much more.

The love affair of the heart and the brain

Recent years have seen a new understanding of how the brain and the heart interact in a complex and dynamic relationship. At one time psychologists believed that emotions were only mental expressions generated by the brain alone. However, we know now that emotions have as much to do with the body as they do with the brain and both impact and inform the other in a symbiotic dance of motion and emotion. Science has proved that the heart has its own nervous system, although it is an integrated system. The heart sends information to the brain, which influences how the brain functions. The heart sends information via the nervous system up through the lower brain centres and right up through the limbic brain, (the emotional processing centre) and through to the neo-cortex (the highest decision making levels in our brain). The brain gets it's information from the heart and there is always more information coming from the heart to the brain than the other way around.

Another way that the heart communicates with the brain is through the hormonal system. The heart was reclassified as an endocrine or hormonal gland in 1983 when a hormone produced and released by the heart called Atrial Natriuretic Factor (ANF) was isolated. This hormone exerts its effects widely: on the blood vessels themselves, on the kidneys and the adrenal glands and on a large number of regulatory regions in the brain. Other hormones produced by the heart are norepinephrine and dopamine, (neurotransmitters once thought to be produced only by neurons in the brain and ganglia outside the heart). More recently still, it was discovered that the heart also secretes oxytocin, commonly referred to as the "love" or "bonding hormone". Oxytocin is well known for its functions in childbirth and lactation; however, recent evidence shows that this hormone is also involved in cognition, tolerance, adaptation and complex sexual and maternal behaviours. It also seems to play a part in the learning of social cues and the establishment of enduring relationships. Remarkably, concentrations of oxytocin in the heart are as high as those found in the brain.

Perhaps the most exciting way that the heart communicates with the brain is energetically. The heart is an electrical organ producing by far the strongest source of bio-electricity in our bodies. Forty to sixty times more powerful than the brain. This permeates every single cell in our body and is strong enough that it creates an electro magnetic field that extends around our body into space about three to four feet. Think of it like a 360 degree invisible field around our physical form. The frequencies in this field are always changing and modulating according to how we feel. In essence, how we feel produces an an informational field of energy around our entire body that is being produced and broadcast by the heart. This emotional state of being is being felt and picked up on by everyone we meet or come into contact with. If we are feeling upset, angry or frustrated, it produces an incoherent spectrum – chaos in the field. If we feel heart based emotions of kindness, care and appreciation that field changes into coherent emotion. The Institute of HeartMath found that the rhythmic beating patterns of the heart are reflective of changes in emotional states and that they align with emotions in real time. These natural fluctuations in heart rate are known as heart-rate variability, which is an important factor in determining your health and well being. I tend to think of them much like the choreography of a dance. Where the mood is tense, stressed, dark or brooding the signature moves will be sharp, jagged, spiky and chaotic. Where the mood is loving, open, warm and peacefully relaxed the moves reflect this by being smooth, more even, wave-like, ordered, flowing and gentle.

Essentially, the more we can live in a loving heart centred way, the more we produce those fluid flowing wavelike oscillations of coherence. This in turn leads us to long term attitude shifts, well being and improvements in being able to manage our emotions.

What is truly exciting with all this research is that we have the ability to change the hearts' rhythmic patterns by making a conscious choice to do so. Whenever you shift your focus to the area of your heart and deliberately choose to feel positive emotions of love, kindness, gratitude, compassion or a deep caring, you rapidly induce a state of increased coherence. The message that "all is well" is sent to the brain, which serves to reinforce this feeling and self generated emotional shift, making it easier to sustain. In essence, every time you choose to focus loving emotions towards yourself, you create a divine loving loop of health, wellness, joy and harmony. Just as you can create and generate a downward spiral of discontent and unhappiness, you can also create an upward spiral of ever evolving love and joy. This is powerful because it gives you ownership and control with how you choose and most desire to feel. For years many people have been told that there is nothing they can do to manage depression, disease or autoimmune conditions. Medication has been the first line of defence with little or no other choices recommended. However, slowly and surely the medical system is becoming more aware that our thoughts play an important role in how we manage our health. With the science to back this up we truly have the power to take responsibility for feeling the best we can be!

The thing is that we all "know" this already. We know that compassion and care makes us feel on top of the world. We have all felt the emotions of fear as they course through our body in a wave of heightened emotion, stress, tension, blind panic and anger. We inherently know what feels good and whole to us and what doesn't. And yet, for so long, loving our body and ourself has been more of a whim or a nice idea if only we could remember to do it. What I am suggesting here is that loving you becomes your number one priority in your life. That you seek to love and take care of yourself in everything you do and wherever you go. That you watch what words you use when talking or describing yourself and others. That you treat your body kindly and with a reverent loving touch. That you take time for you and slow down. That you listen to the passionate beating of your heart's desires and that you take them seriously as if your life depended on it. It does! There is only one of you in this vast Universe. The fact that you are here is a miracle in itself. How you live your extraordinary life depends entirely on the relationship you have with yourself every day of your life. You get to choose. You can choose to suffer and pull yourself down. You can make your body wrong and decide to punish it. Or you can choose to stand by and with yourself every moment of every day. Like a proud, wilful and fiercely indomitable spirit you can champion your dreams and ride on the wings of your beauty, strength and loving heart.

What are you here for if not that? What is your life all about if not to embody it fully, wholeheartedly and completely? You are here now. If you do not step into the warm embrace of your beautiful being, no one else can. How can anyone else get in if you can't or won't? Stop living next door to your body and decide to fully inhabit your own spectacular shape and form. You are not wrong, broken, bad or not good enough. That's just a story that has been passed down to you by those who were also told this fable and believed the myth. Come back to the loving wisdom and intelligence of your beautiful heart and listen to the soft gentle whispers of your soul calling out to you to love you. When will you decide to commit and connect to the most important person in your life – YOU! Everything else comes from this sweet spot of love. Every other life you touch blossoms under the dappled sunlight of your own enduring love. Every other relationship you have is built on the qualities that you know how to embody – trust, compassion, kindness, love, conscious choices and mindful moments of meaning. Come back, wake up and remember who you really are. Take baby steps of action on your dreams and always whisper to yourself the words that you most want to hear. So many of us were taught that loving ourselves was selfish and that we should put our own needs, desires and wants last. If that belief was working we would have a world full of people who are happy, healthy and living their wildest dreams. The truth is that it doesn't work. It has never worked and it's time to reclaim your power, purpose, passion and presence. I spent far too long living on the sidelines of my life. I held back. I didn't believe that I had anything useful to offer or that anyone would even be interested. And as I disappeared from my own view I disappeared from my life. And for what? Did my lack of loving myself or acknowledging my authentic truth make the world a better, happier place? Did I add joy and laughter to the people I loved? Quite the opposite was true as I became more insular, closed off and full of pain. The sad thing is that the world will miss you if you're not there. You will miss you. Life will have lost one of its most precious shining stars. There is one moment in life that stretches out for your entire lifetime. It's the moment that you're in right now. And this moment always invites you to fall deeper in love with life and you exactly as it is. The question is, will you?

If you truly loved your body...(Body confidence coaching exercise)

Imagine that you really love and cherish your body so much that you always strive to nurture and express your feelings and give yourself the best that you can.

The following questions ask you about what it means to truly love, honour and respect your body and yourself.

Go with the first thoughts or images that come into your mind.

1. If you truly loved your body (and self) what would you tell you?

2. If you truly loved your body (and self) what would you stop doing?
3. If you truly loved your body (and self) what would you begin doing?
4. If you truly loved your body (and self) what foods would you choose to eat?
5. If you truly loved your body (and self) what and how much exercise would you do?
6. If you truly loved your body (and self) how much sleep would you make sure you got every night?
7. If you truly loved your body (and self) what present would you give you?
8. If you truly loved your body (and self) how would you relax?
9. If you truly loved your body (and self) how might your life be different?
10. If you truly loved your body (and self) what feelings would this generate within you?
11. If you truly loved your body (and self) what would be unacceptable in your behaviour?

When you love your body you are always home!

There are many reasons that we choose to vacate our bodies and therefore our lives. Sometimes early childhood trauma or shock makes us jump out of our body and never come back. Other times it's because we believe that somehow the body we have isn't good enough or resembles someone else's body that we believe to be better. And so we become homeless. We may find temporary accommodation in the vast recesses of our mind or spend our lives jumping in and out of other people's lives as we seek to avoid our own. Ultimately, the body will always try to bring your spirit home. Your body needs you to be present within its gentle and loving embrace. It needs you to help steer its course and fulfil the agreement you made long, long ago. The agreement for your spirit to experience full embodiment on this earth. The truth is that when you love your body and your life, you are always home. You are also never alone – how can you be? You have YOU! The illusion of feeling separate melts away and you know that all you have to do is to reach out for you again and again. The world needs you to love you – now more than ever. The Universe is constantly calling you to live your fullest, happiest and most loving life. It will work with you every step of the way on your journey – if you allow it. When you love you, you treat yourself well. The old behaviours become unacceptable as you love yourself too much to hurt you anymore (or allow others to hurt you!) And from this place you can let anything happen. You may find yourself feeling the urge to actually write that book that's been rumbling around in your head for years. You may start to eat a little more kindly. You may make significant life changes or none at all as you realise your life is just magical the way it is (you just hadn't noticed it before). There is a gentle opening up of possibilities and potential that becomes exciting rather than fearful and full of doubt. You desire to please you and take care of you and this is rewarded by the sweetest of feelings and a gentle unfolding of health and harmony. Rather like the Northern Lights, you allow yourself to flow and move with the brightest of colours as you sweep across the landscape of your brilliant body. For me, it was a dawning realisation that it if I didn't decide to change my relationship with me and love all of who I am then nothing else really mattered. No one else could make me happy. Only I could do that. I realised that all of my disconnection and unacceptance of me only led to a lifetime of regret and "If only's!" Whilst my distressful relationship with food provided me with the excuse to escape and hide from my feelings, they didn't bring me the joy I truly hungered for and craved. Ultimately, I couldn't see the point anymore in holding back or tiptoeing around the edges of my skin because I didn't want to see me or have anything to do with me. I realised that all of the books I had inside of my heart would never get written. All of the joy and adventures that I could have would never be experienced. All of the people that I could help or share joy with would never come into being. All that I would leave my life with was fear, doubt, insecurity and treating myself unkindly. I really hope that you hear my words loud in your head and your heart as you read them. Life isn't a rehearsal. This is it! We are living this magical and challenging dance one step at a time. We can't get it back, all we can do is to learn the choreography and keep practicing until loving ourselves becomes second nature; as if there was never a time when we didn't adore the very bones of our beautiful bodies. And when you decide to choose love as your soulmate, you open the doors for everyone around you to do the same. You change the stories of the past as you continually write the one you desire to live in the moment. The most powerful thing about this is that your radiance and love is felt and picked up on by everyone else around you. So not only do you change yourself but you also change the global coherence and consciousness of the world.

Feel your body and love it anyway!

The other morning I sat on the edge of my bed and rested my hands on my belly. I looked down at the soft roundness that nestled beneath my fingers and I breathed in deeply. I ran one finger gently over the long scar that was still visible from a surgery I had when I was eighteen. I traced the edges where the scar had widened and noticed where it still remained slightly reddened. My past, still clearly etched into my body as a ghostly reminder of that time when I was so poorly. I closed my eyes and gently began to brush my belly lightly with my hands. In my mind I imagined that I was brushing away every unkind word that I had ever said about my belly – about my body. As my hands continually lightly caressed my skin, I breathed in deeply and gave thanks to my belly for enduring the pain of the past. As I brushed away the years, I felt such a deep kindness and love rise up from deep within every cell of my being. In the past I would have tried to avoid even looking at my scar condemning it as ugly. But, there in that moment I felt an indescribable peace and love for my wonderful belly that had been through so much. Romancing your body with unconditional love means that you make a choice and commitment to be present for and with your body no matter what. When your days are dark and full of confusion or sadness, you turn to your body first and wrap it up in soft whispers of love. You refuse to enter the anxious chambers of your thoughts and instead invite those worrying thoughts into the soft current of your breath. Drawing each and every negative or fearful thought or belief down into the warmth and safety of your beloved belly. Here, you can cradle the fears, the doubts and the worries until they feel loved enough to loosen their controlling grip and flow easily into the next moment. And suddenly you are free! Free from the chains that have bound you or conditioned you into believing you needed to be something or someone that you are not. Free from having to lock your feelings down along with your life force. You are free to walk in your own magic, beauty, fire and presence and know that it's okay to sparkle! Free to create, dance, laugh, take a chance, ride a moonbeam, create a fairytale, speak your truth, revel in your passion, say "No," say "Yes," say "I don't know." Freedom takes many shapes and forms but you will know it when it is there because you will feel it. What does it feel like? LOVE!

This type of love takes practice and a willingness to be there for you. It requires that you show up every day, even in the smallest of ways and really notice and be with you. What if you simply allowed yourself to love what you love? To tend to the soft animal of your own body with each breath that rises and falls, with every feeling that comes and flows. Your wisdom is beyond measure and it's always there for you stored in every experience, every memory and every emotion of your life. Take time every day to tune in and listen to the callings of your inner knowing. Close your eyes, place your hand over your heart, and breathe in the moment. Exhale and thank the past. Every single experience, thought, idea, action, event and feeling has led you to this moment. Nothing has ever been wasted in your life. Every single experience has value beyond words, even though you may feel unsure about what that is. It doesn't matter. Just the fact that you are here reading these words speaks volumes. Somehow, you got here. That's all that matters. The practice of unconditional love takes time, but is much faster than you might think. Don't be fooled by the small scared child's voice of the subconscious mind that will try to tell you that you are not lovable or that you will never do this. It's just an old "story." It has no power or truth over you anymore. Those words were never yours; they belonged to an ancient myth from an ancient time, passed down through your family line. Be kind to these old treasures. They served a purpose once. Learn from what they have taught you and where they have brought you. Without them, you wouldn't be here, back in the arms of your own belonging.

The last goodbye

Your body is the one relationship that has been with you since (and before) your birth and will be the last relationship in your life. Your body is the final goodbye, your last attachment to this world in physical form. Some day we will all make that journey and leave these precious vehicles. But until that day, make yourself a promise that you will live all the days of your wonderful life fully, passionately, lovingly and wholeheartedly. Promise yourself that you will take care of and love your amazing body. Make the commitment to fall in love with you more each day and make it unacceptable to hurt or self-sabotage you even for another minute. Then you will have truly had all the days of your life.

Then you will have been here for all that life had to offer; the great, the not so great, the wonder, the pain, the joy and the sorrow. Many people spend most of their lives trying to leave their body as they try to avoid feeling what they feel, knowing what they know or doing what they really don't want to do. Much of their life is simply one long drawn out goodbye. It's easy to leave; there are many routes and many ways. It's harder to stay but it's where the joy lives! So, run towards yourself, arms open wide, heart beating in excitement, your mind full of curiosity about who you are and who you are becoming. Don't hold back. There's nothing to wait for anymore. You are here. You only have to turn around, smile and let yourself in and allow you to be loved by YOU! And when, at last your time comes to say goodbye to your beautiful body, you can leave knowing that you have truly lived (in the words of Mary Oliver) your one wild and precious life.

FOR MORE INFORMATION ON ASTRID'S WORKSHOPS, TRAINING AND COACHING:

www.instituteforbodyconfidencecoaching.com

www.astridlonghurst.com

www.chakranetics.com

REFERENCES

Emmons, R. A., & McCullough, M. E. (2003)

Faulds Dana - Poem Awakening Now http://www.mindfullivingprograms.com/resources_poetry.php

Oliver Mary The Wild Geese, http://www.rjgeib.com/thoughts/geese/geese.html

Pinkola Estes Clarissa, Women who run with the wolves, Ballantine Books; Reissue edition (November 27, 1996)

Worrall Simon, National Geographic Magazine. http://news.nationalgeographic.com/2015/01/150128-big-bang-universe-supernova-astrophysics-health-space-ngbooktalk/ January 28, 2015

ACKNOWLEDGMENTS

There are so many people that I am grateful to on my own journey to loving and accepting my body. Here is just a snapshot of those I would like to thank – I wish I could name you all, however, please just know that you are in my heart and have my deepest gratitude.

I would like to thank first and foremost all of my wonderful clients who have allowed me to share their body stories in this book. I am deeply grateful to you all – you have taught me so much. Thank you! My heartfelt thanks and love go to my sister, Helen, who remarked that perhaps I had written Romancing your body just for her as she embarked on her own healing journey with her body. Yes, my love it is for YOU! Thank you for being such a beautiful sister!

Thank you to my amazing editing team especially Loz-Ann McCarthy who worked tirelessly on formatting and helping me with the "technicalities" of bringing this book to life! Also for the beautiful photograph that graces the front cover. I am forever grateful. My heartfelt gratitude goes to my lovely soul sister Kate who saw through my pain and believed in me and loved me anyway! Such a friendship forged in childhood that has evolved over the years to be a source of so much joy and love. I thank you for being there! Thanks go to my amazing soul sisters Meg and Cassie. So many hours of wonder, magic and exploring life's journey - thank you for the magic.

Where would I be without the indomitable spirit and friendship of Lynn. Never above you, never below you, always with you. And to John - Your passion and zest for life will remain forever in my heart.

To the people who are no longer alive in my life – know that you will always be alive in my heart and in my gratitude.

Finally, thanks go to my own body who has been the greatest teacher in my life. Thank you for giving my soul such a wonderful "home" to live in all these years. Thank you for helping me to learn how to love and accept myself, move through the pain and help others to do the same.

And to the readers of this book – I thank you all for being open to the possibility and very real truth that when we fall in love with ourselves, life falls in love with us! Thank you for your courage, beauty and wisdom as we travel this path together!

ABOUT THE AUTHOR

Astrid Longhurst

Astrid is the founder and CEO of the Institute for Body Confidence Coaching. (A transformational body confidence coaching training programme). She is a world class body confidence coach and also a mindful movement and energy psychology expert. She teaches her own unique mindful sacred energy movement meditation classes (Chakranetics - Energy Medicine Fitness). She is also the author of the highly acclaimed book "Body Confidence," published by Penguin. Romancing your body is her second book.

Astrid was the first plus size fitness presenter on UK National Television (GMTV) and also one of the first generation plus size models. She has helped pioneer the way for women to look and feel fabulous at every shape, size and age!

Astrid's passion is to help people heal their relationship with their body and live their happiest and most authentic life! Her vision is to forever change the way we see and relate to our body, enabling us to live empowered, dynamic, happy, healthy, fabulous and fulfilled lives in a body that we love, cherish, respect and adore! Astrid's work is at the leading edge of a movement which is inspiring a whole new awakening around the relationship we have with our body, ourselves, our world and what it means to be fully alive and engaged with our true purpose in life.

Her story, passion for life, expertise, warmth and charisma make her perhaps one of the most motivational coaches of our time.

Astrid is also an inspirational speaker at many health & wellness events including The Vitality Show (London) The Ideal Home Show (London), Mind body spirit show at The RDS (Dublin).

For more information on Astrid's workshops, personal coaching & events please contact:

body_confidence@yahoo.co.uk
www.astridlonghurst.com
www.chakranetics.com
www.instituteforbodyconfidencecoaching.com

www.astridlonghurst.com

Printed in Great Britain
by Amazon

46880278R00154